QUANT
AIKIDO

"In language that is both lyrical and clear, Richard shows us the underlying unity of creation. He does this through the perspectives of quantum physics, music, and the Japanese martial art of Aikido. These multiple perspectives highlight the underlying unity between ourselves and the universe at large."

BOB NOHA, 7TH DAN, CHIEF INSTRUCTOR OF
AIKIDO OF PETALUMA AND COAUTHOR OF
AIKIDO: THE ART OF TRANSFORMATION

"Richard Moon Sensei is a leader who has contributed greatly to the world of Aikido for many years. I believe his new book, *Quantum Aikido*, will be a gateway that opens a new door for those who practice Aikido in the future."

HIROSHI IKEDA, 8TH DAN, FOUNDER AND
CHIEF INSTRUCTOR OF BOULDER AIKIKAI INC.
AND VICE PRESIDENT OF AIKIDO SHIMBOKUKAI ORGANIZATION

"If you are interested in a transformative path involving a deep connection with self and others, an embodied spiritual practice, and unifying with a universal energy, I highly recommend *Quantum Aikido*."

RICHARD STROZZI-HECKLER, 7TH DAN,
AUTHOR OF *EMBODYING THE MYSTERY*

"*Quantum Aikido* is a brilliant overview of the power of blending the art of attention with the science of action. It is a must-read guide to learning how to dance in an emerging world where it is becoming harder to hear the music."

ROBERT H. LENGEL, AUTHOR OF *THE FRONT PORCH REVOLUTION*

"In an age where we are drowning in information on how to be happy and live healthier—yet suffering from dis-ease in both arenas—Richard Moon's experience-based wisdom offers a missing link. The answers have always been within us, and *Quantum Aikido* paves a path to reconnect with what the body already knows: that what we seek—for both inner and collective reconciliation—is not far, but lives encoded in the intuitive intelligence of our movement, breath, and energy."

EMILIA ELISABET LAHTI, PH.D., AUTHOR OF *GENTLE POWER*

"Richard Moon shows how our individual spirit can connect with broader energies by replacing confrontation with a comfort born of acceptance and open curiosity. This is an astonishing and profoundly instructive book."

PETER GOODMAN, PUBLISHER AT STONE BRIDGE PRESS

"In *Quantum Aikido*, Richard Moon has captured light in a bottle! Simplicity itself: when facing challenges, let yourself feel more. When we sink open, we feel vibrant universal energy rising in response. Further releasing into that wave of intensity, we receive the natural flow of intuitive wisdom and spontaneous creativity. Releasing into energetic presence, we merge with the unified field of limitless awareness and awaken as one. Thank you, Moon Sensei."

CHRISTOPHER THORSEN, AIKIDO TEACHER AND FOUNDER OF INQUIRY INTO CONSCIOUSNESS AND QUANTUM EDGE

"Richard is a committed teacher and investigator, daring to push the envelope and attempting to discover deeper truths. The cutting edge of quantum physics and its role in our lives is a new and interesting frontier. Although we don't know where such research and theories will ultimately end up, if it helps to improve people's lives and increase their effectiveness in relating to the forces of life, I support Richard's contributions to the effort."

PETER RALSTON, AUTHOR OF *ENDING UNNECESSARY SUFFERING* AND *THE ART OF MASTERY*

QUANTUM AIKIDO

THE POWER OF HARMONY

A Sacred Planet Book

RICHARD MOON

PARK STREET PRESS
ROCHESTER, VERMONT

Park Street Press
One Park Street
Rochester, Vermont 05767
www.ParkStPress.com

Park Street Press is a division of Inner Traditions International

Sacred Planet Books are curated by Richard Grossinger, Inner Traditions editorial board member and cofounder and former publisher of North Atlantic Books. The Sacred Planet collection, published under the umbrella of the Inner Traditions family of imprints, includes works on the themes of consciousness, cosmology, alternative medicine, dreams, climate, permaculture, alchemy, shamanic studies, oracles, astrology, crystals, hyperobjects, locutions, and subtle bodies.

Cataloging-in-Publication Data for this title is available from the Library of Congress

ISBN 978-1-64411-977-8 (print)
ISBN 978-1-64411-978-5 (ebook)

Printed and bound in the United States by Lake Book Manufacturing, LLC

10 9 8 7 6 5 4 3 2 1

Text design by Kira Kariakin and layout by Alfonso Reyes G.

This book was typeset in Garamond Premier Pro, Arquitecta, Aviano, Cantoria MT and Nirmala UI

To send correspondence to the author of this book, mail a first-class letter to the author c/o Inner Traditions, One Park Street, Rochester, VT 05767, and we will forward the communication, or contact the author directly at **moonsensei@gmail.com**.

Scan the QR code and save 25% at InnerTraditions.com. Browse over 2,000 titles on spirituality, the occult, ancient mysteries, new science, holistic health, and natural medicine.

To those who have gone before
The Aiki Kami, the Divine Spirit of Aikido
Morihei Ueshiba Osensei, founder of Aikido
Robert Nadeau, Osensei's student and my instructor

To those who have walked with me
Stephen Samuels, Chris Thorsen, and so many others

For all that has been given to me
And for those who follow

CONTENTS

ℛ

PART ONE
ENTERING THE QUANTUM WORLD

PART TWO
AIKIDO: OSENSEI'S PROCESS

FOREWORD

Douglas Stone

I remember clear as yesterday the first time I met Richard. It was the mid-1990s, and I was teaching conflict resolution at Harvard Law School while doing some consulting on the side. We were both part of the staff working on a weeklong mediation project in Cyprus, along with four others. Cyprus was then, and as of this writing still is, a divided community; the northern part of the Mediterranean island nation is dominated by Turkish Cypriots, while the southern part is dominated by Greek Cypriots.

At the time of our project, the two communities were fully divided; communication and interaction across the "green line" was logistically and politically difficult (or impossible). Our task was to bring twenty members of each community together and to facilitate conversation between them. This kind of project is called "track two diplomacy" because we were dealing not with politicians and diplomats, but with community leaders. Our goal was to foster greater understanding and trust between two communities that had many reasons not to trust each other.

Most of us on the team had not met prior to arriving on the island. The day before the conference began, five of us had been planning long into the night. Work with divided communities is often stressful and uncertain. We brainstormed idea after idea, but couldn't settle on a final agenda for Day One. Richard's flight arrived late, and by the time he made his entrance around midnight, the rest of us were exhausted and cranky. Only one person on our team had ever met Richard. When he walked in, he was smiling and calm, and had a mischievous gleam in his eye. Sensing the room's energy, he made a remark along the lines of, "If you look to the totality, what's wrong points to what's right. Envision what tomorrow would be if it were great." Then with a laugh, he added, "Of course, I could be wrong. Anything can happen. I should introduce myself. I'm Richard Moon."

My spirits lifted. Our new arrival was not just confident, he was also funny. He knew how to change the mood in a room with a single observation or question. He was just the right guy for this moment. Whatever surprises were in store for us over the next week, Richard, through the harmonious power of Aikido, would know what to say and do. And he did. His presence and wisdom reassured the Cypriot participants just as that same presence and wisdom had reassured me that first night. Feeling safe and seen, participants felt more comfortable taking on the difficult work of reconciliation and understanding across differences.

As I've gotten to know Richard better these past thirty years, both professionally and personally, he's remained true to that first impression. He possesses an unusual mix of deep confidence and self-effacing humility grounded in an almost aggressive curiosity about everything around him. He makes choices with intention and assurance, yet he's always willing to rethink the direction he's moving in, to try something new. This is the power harmony gifts to a person.

Over the years, I've noticed that more than a few of the folks drawn to Richard regard him as possessing a kind of magic. If he isn't a full-fledged wizard of some sort, surely he's no mere mortal either. Is there some portal, some river of wisdom, he is able to access that the rest of us can't? When people spend time with Richard, even the most skeptical among them begin to wonder.

For the record, Richard is not a wizard. He's a person like you and me (I'm almost certain). His power to move people beyond themselves is not based on some supernatural enlightenment but resides in his very humanness—his studious intelligence, his compassion, his insight. He sees the world differently from most people, and yet he is able to see each of us just as we want to be seen. Because of that mix of sensibilities and skills, Richard is a guy people want to learn from.

His power comes from his training and unique vision. His devotion to study is why people see him as a teacher. Like everything about Richard, his teaching—whether about Aikido or communication or life—allows him to see the universal that encompasses seeming opposites. Even as his students see him as a master, he sees himself as a student. He's not perched before us as the wise man, but helps us parse the wisdom in our own thoughts and experiences. His curiosity inspires our own.

Richard, as a student of Aikido, means what we all mean by the word *Aikido*, but he also means a lot more. To him, it's a way of seeing the world and a way of being in and of the world. As he writes: "Aikido, commonly described as a Japanese martial art, is rather a larger study. Transcending the paradigm of martial arts as quantum mechanics did with physics and jazz with music, Aikido was described by the founder of the art as the 'realization of love.'"

The rest of the book, in my view, is a series of elaborations and variations on that theme.

Speaking of variations, Richard, you won't be surprised to learn, is also a musician. He plays in a range of musical styles, but he lives his life as an improviser, like a jazz musician. Given life's fathomless uncertainties, there really isn't any other way one can live, though many of us still try to follow the sheet music.

But Richard knows there isn't any alternative, and so, that which is written here originates from the creativity of improvisation. *Quantum Aikido: The Power of Harmony* is written down, of course, but it's not sheet music. Although rigorously organized, the writing and ideas channel the spirit of jazz. Some sections read like a dare: *I know you're with me, but we're going further in, further out. Are you ready?* Other parts have a bell-like clarity: *Really, it's that simple, folks.* Sometimes Richard's teachings take us up to the end of the road and point the way, encouraging ever-greater exploration. Other times, Richard—being the definition of the word *sensei*, or "one who has gone before"—has gone somewhere before us, metabolized the lessons, and shares what he found on his journey.

Either way, through the teachings in this book, you'll be challenged and enlightened, and perhaps changed. Sometimes you'll agree, sometimes you'll disagree. But if you open up to it, you'll always marvel. That is what this book has to offer, just like life.

DOUGLAS STONE has been a law lecturer at Harvard Law School for thirty-five years and is a coauthor of the international bestseller *Difficult Conversations: How to Discuss What Matters Most.*

PREFACE

Once upon a time, when the hint of dawn was on the horizon, the child of human consciousness, awakened from a dream by mysterious echoes, wandered out of the darkness in exploration of an unknown universe. Drawn out of the shadows toward the source of light, this awakening awareness responds, even now, to the beckoning of whispers, energies expanding the threshold of consciousness. The winds of imagination, like chimes calling or the guidance of a distant chant, appear from the energy of a changing universe and take the form of disturbance or disruption rippling through human consciousness.

The force of disturbance is creativity itself. The unfolding universal energy that underlies existence emerges as the flow of life force. Across varying degrees of consciousness, an alive system—a unified field of functions that produce the experience of life, many of these unconscious, and all aspects of aliveness encapsulated in the word *life*—is always adjusting in response to a changing universe. Seeking the path home amidst the incoherent complexity found in the various explanations of life, human awareness discovers that little seems to make sense. Instead, as understanding grows, every answer highlights a larger incoherence, question, or mystery.

The ancient teachings to which we have access appear to contradict both each other and the unfolding knowledge of the sciences . . . at first. However, as we step back to look from a certain distance, a picture emerges from the seemingly chaotic painting. The world of a million brushstrokes dissolves, distilling a singular image of the whole out of the overwhelming complexity. Through the changing prism of consciousness, components merge as an interconnected network, a unified field in the realm of the spirit.

The stories that follow come from a single source that is, at the same time, the whole of creation. The winds of the mystery whistle through creation, whispering a call to evolving consciousness.

Wisdom crystallizes in the crack between the two worlds, that of past knowing and that which arises out of looking into the unknown. Attention follows the call of exploration down the path of wonder; we are uncertain of the path's purpose and yet unable to quiet the mysterious attraction. The mystery is always sharing its intelligence in a language closer to feeling than thought, closer to music than words, inviting the unity of diverse creation to enjoy the dance.

INTRODUCTION

L ife beyond time and place magnetically moves toward pleasure and away from pain, toward joy and away from anguish. That is the medium through which the nervous system transmits its guiding message. As the human brain develops it is driven by an intangible force, whether described as pressure, energy, an entity, or a field. Human knowledge evolves to fulfill the innate desire of every being. Everyone wants to feel better, and no one wants to feel worse.

Spiritual development influences the single most critical factor in the unfolding destinies of individuals and of the species, the spirit with which one enters each moment. Attitude, always a determinant of success, is hypercritical in the first instance of any engagement, on the leading edge. Just as an infant's earliest moments and first impressions after birth are seminal, the cumulative experience created at the dawn of each moment will pattern the neural pathways that enshrine life's destiny.

The quality of spirit, attitude, or courage with which one enters each moment of life may seem random, yet it forms as the result of a process. Learning, the primary life drive supporting survival, requires emptying one's cup, an open willingness to enter the unknown. Letting go of the known, or embracing any new experience, may be uncomfortable at first. As when entering a hot bath, it may take time to adjust, to acclimatize and appreciate what is being offered.

In a sense, with every moment we enter a new land where we require new language, skills, and knowledge of custom. Once we are familiar with the language and customs, a new country seems much more enjoyable. Both analogies hold true with entry into the formless study of the power of living in harmony with the universe of energy.

The brave choice to generate a spirit of harmony upon entry into the unknown turns our experience toward enjoyment, exploration, and learning. Training to listen instead of resisting defensively allows the disturbance of new experience to unfold as information and guidance. In the moment of entry into the unknown, intentionally choosing a spirit of learning, of inquiry, of wonder and exploration reverberates in growth and development, increasing the likelihood of successfully negotiating the events that make up life.

Feeling better and enjoying a more fulfilling life experience also means gaining heightened sensory acuity and increased conscious experience of sensation. Or in other words, inescapably, this heightened acuity and experience exists in interactive duality with the feeling that one is experiencing more or better. When we increase attention to the signals of the alive system, this informs decisions directing life experience on its path. Listened to holistically, the signals of the senses guide intelligence to know what to do or change, what trail to follow, or how to blaze one. As the passion of the life force explores its fulfillment, it leads impulses, urges, feelings, and drives to surface into consciousness, where, properly aligned with the whole, they propel life to a fulfilling completion.

Consciousness, a word with an ever-expanding definition, equates at the simplest level of understanding with sensory awareness, the thinking-feeling-knowing aspects of being. The science of anesthesia studies how to turn consciousness *down*. Spiritual awareness studies how to turn it *up*. Spiritual practice deals with pain and pleasure in life by feeling them *more*: feeling pain better, feeling pleasure better, feeling better.

Though it can be challenging to intentionally point attention toward feeling discomfort, feeling is the path to experiencing energy as intelligence. The messages transmitted by the neural system suggest intentional action to manage or direct thoughts, feelings, and awareness. Only by our feeling the energy or pressure that may at first seem uncomfortable, can the messages be decoded as guidance indicating what might correct, or improve, a given situation. Feeling better is not a self-centered or insignificant process but rather indicates an intelligent, harmonious response to an ever-changing universe, a response that expands as consciousness experiences it.

Feeling better means increasing sensitivity to the spirit, attitude, or mood one engenders. Here, the word *spirit* points to the source and quality of vitality. The spirit one lives in and radiates can be "colored in" using many terms: state of being, attitude, mood, humor, affect, mindset, temperament, or operating place. Spirit is the function through which one listens to and expresses relationship with creation, harmonious or otherwise.

Gaining power is one thing. Using it intelligently is another. The process of paying attention to experience brings the quality of spirit into the realm of conscious influence. The internal process of aligning experience with changing meaning is mutable, accessible, and potentially within the realm of influence of the focus of attention. The external world is largely outside of the control of any one individual. Though it can be influenced to some degree, it is best influenced by Aikido's fundamental process, correcting the discord in one's own mind first, rather than attempting to correct others from an out-of-sorts state of being.

Enjoying life and living in joy are to some degree mysteriously volitional, because in some unknown way, enjoyment is a product of intent. Imagine if "feeling better" could produce effective function beyond present imagination—which would be as dramatically revolutionary as the shift into quantum theory was for physics. Imagine a "quantum shift" in creating mastery, comparable to the exponential transformation from conventional weapons to the thermonuclear devices of today. Only, imagine that intensity of power directed not toward destructive ends but rather intentionally brought to bear in the spirit of loving protection and peaceful reconciliation. Imagine if the world were to wage peace as intensely as it wages war.

THE SORCERER'S APPRENTICE

Goethe's *The Sorcerer's Apprentice* tells the story of an apprentice left with chores by his master. Tired of his tasks, the apprentice uses magic he fails to fully understand, and enchants a broom to fetch water for him. The broom does the work but cannot be stopped, causing the room to flood. The apprentice tries to stop the broom by splitting it with an axe, but each piece becomes a whole broom, exacerbating the problem. The sorcerer returns just in time and breaks the spell, warning his apprentice that only a master should invoke powerful spirits.

Technology splits the broom, reinforcing and amplifying the power of patterns regardless of their quality. To apply power intelligently requires the development of more than just cerebral data processing. Tempering the spirit activates the higher angels of being, enabling us to feel better and not worse, thus reinforcing harmony in the world.

THE SHIFT

This second
has already passed
as
has this one
The moment is so fleeting
yet
The now is eternal

As the twentieth century began, a dimensional shift in human consciousness showed up through quantum mechanics, jazz, and Aikido, among other portals. Aikido, commonly described as a Japanese martial art, is rather a larger study. Transcending the paradigm of martial arts as quantum mechanics did with physics and jazz with music, Aikido was described by the founder of the art as the "realization of love."

Often referred to as the way of harmony, and sometimes as the art of peace, Aikido is a unification of the following three elements: *Do,* or a way of aligning; *Ai*, or harmonious relationship; and *Ki*, or universal energy. The metaphor translates to harmoniously handling the changes and challenges of daily life by distilling and applying principles from the martial realm to creativity in the business of living.

Quantum mechanics, jazz, and Aikido opened doorways into the present zeitgeist, shifting the paradigm of consciousness so that it could imagine and perceive possibilities that have always been present but are only now surfacing. Quantum mechanics opens a world that could turn out to be either the wish-bestowing genie's lamp or Pandora's box. Enter Aikido, which offers the spiritual power to align humanity through its use of technology in service of the realization of love.

The way of harmony provides an alternative to the continuum of fighting or giving up, and is a process that can reconcile the world. Aikido's cultivation of the spirit of reconciliation absorbs and utilizes the energy of a situation, be it change or violent attack, to create spontaneous resolution, which can lead to innovative solutions in any study or discipline. The principles of Aikido teach improvisational creativity in response to the unexpected, creating technique in the moment, at high speed and under pressure, at a level of effectiveness beyond present imagination.

The speed and intensity of change happening today overwhelm present societal structures and forms of thought. Without creativity, a culture remains stuck in the past and find change terrifying. In overwhelm, mood falls victim to the winds and storms. When in a bad mood or feeling "out" of sorts, people act *out* by losing their temper, or act *in* by giving up in exasperation. People who are scared out of their wits, individually or in groups, attack each other instead of the problems they face. Though this phenomenon is not new, if we consider the population curve, resource and ecological pressures, and the explosion of technology, we see that responding to change has increasingly become a critically dangerous channel or, if done intelligently, a potentially enlightening opportunity.

Aikido, resonant with the mysteries of quantum mechanics, is a study of energy. To highlight the connection between Aikido and quantum mechanics invokes the oft-missed transformational magic Aikido offers. The way of harmony, where invoking joy as the greatest treasure, leads to the creation of a fulfilling life and the completion of one's bestowed mission.

Through the growth, development, and fulfillment of each individual, the art of Aikido invokes the creation of a beautiful world as an amalgam of the individuals who make up that world. Developing and radiating harmonious spirit creates a magnetic field of loving protection, cultivating reconciliation in the world. One creates a beautiful world primarily through "being the change one wishes to see."

Harmony starts when we connect with our relationship to the internal experience of the universal energy rush as it floods the alive system in response to any external stimulation. The practice of harmony with universal energy begins simply by aligning breathing with the universal pulse, which appears in the alive system as the impulse to breathe.

Harmony, like all virtues, begins at home. Harmony with the breath, listening to the impulse to breathe, is a simple, accessible, tangible first step on the road to harmony with the energy that creates the impulse of breath out of the totality of the universe. A harmonious spirit transforms life experience from a struggle to a dance.

PART ONE

ENTERING
THE QUANTUM WORLD

The Whisperings of the Kami

In the vast
emptiness
of Eternity
flows
the energy of
the universal
intelligence

one system
of
divine
creation ensues

in the emptiness
energy and perception
is
the formation
of
our
lives

1

CREATIVITY IS BORN FROM THE FIELD OF POTENTIAL

Haina ia mai ana ka puana
Let the story be told
Tell and retell the story

STORY, SYNAPTIC PATHWAYS, AND SYSTEMS OF THOUGHT

Since the dawn of human consciousness, our ancestors have gazed into the vastness of the night sky, imagining patterns in the stars and creating stories about them. The human brain and being develop through discerning patterns and exploring meaning, all of which drives life's action and thus produces life's outcome. Through connecting seemingly significant data points, and constructing designs and descriptions, brain function attempts to simplify the incomprehensible into a working understanding of WIGO—a phrase coined by Samuel Bois in *The Art of Awareness*—that stands for What Is Going On. The stories we create about what is going on in reality form the decisions and strategies of what to do about it.

Descriptions of experience real or imagined—stories—emerge, making meaning while creating understanding of interaction with the world. The process of making meaning is a semantic transaction that projects experience into language, giving birth to ideologies, beliefs, fables, myths, and legends.

Sharing stories around the fire creates culture, fostering shared understanding, somatic patterns, and synaptic pathways. Culture shapes individuals who, in a reciprocal process, shape the values, principles, and traditions of the social network. Stories develop into systems of thought that individually and collectively create evolving social structures—religious, political, educational, and otherwise.

Stories are based on past experiences, thus they offer an educated viewpoint from which to make intelligent, strategic predictions for future action. Stories encapsulate the basis of a culture's knowledge and serve as repositories thereof. Stories, in other words, function as software programs for life.

From a tiny point in a universe beyond imagination, our senses abstract a minute fraction of experiential reality that can be seen or understood through the lens of attention. The designs of data assemble themselves as information, not just in thought, but in the material world—physiologically, neurologically, and bio-electromagnetically. Selected data is passed to awareness. It is then organized, collated, and systematized through habituated thought patterns and mental models, cultural as well as personal. This process gives birth to story, which then affects the course of our lives as if it were reality.

Every thought, description, idea, and mode of understanding, and most importantly the entire inner dialogue, creates story, with or without one's awareness of it. The implications of the power of story—especially the inner dialogue, or stories repeated internally—reveal hidden power in creating the experience of life. Fashioning the stories that inform life comes out of an essential human need: the need to know what to do. Story, making meaning, describing, and predicting are compelling, virtually compulsive human activities that respond to that need. Though meaning-making may not be thought of as creativity, it is.

FAMILIAR PATHWAYS

Rain washes down a soft dirt hillside, creating gullies along paths of least resistance. The next time it rains, water flows following and reinforcing the same pathways. Physiologically, stories form neural pathways and patterns in the brain. Patterns form out of ideas, images, inner dialogue, and the stories of others, and once these patterns are adopted, they tend to set quickly. Feelings, like thoughts, quickly default down familiar pathways of affect in the form of synaptic signals, shaping persona and character.

As synaptic pathways deepen, stories, positions, and thought patterns, as well as emotional states and responses, fire off semi-mechanically, habituating into a fixed and familiar affect and stance. Once created, neural connections become established patterns, repetitively following and reinforcing the same pathways.

In the process of crystal formation, the first shape that forms as crystallization begins is referred to as the seed crystal. Every aspect that forms following inception tends to match the shape of the seed crystal. In the same way, the first stories, systems of thought, or beliefs become, in effect, a primary model or archetype, the seed crystal on which future stories are based.

From birth onward, the impressionable synaptic system absorbs stories and attitudes, positions and patterns. Early imprints filter out of the vastness that which is valued enough to be noticed. The first pathways we form design what future information will be received and how it will be valued, and ultimately, the quality of the story that will be developed. Early patterns form the foundation of thought structures and tonality of affect, and these patterns habituate before rational thought exists to assess their accuracy and evaluate their usefulness.

It takes considerable intention to challenge belief systems adopted before the development of critical thinking, before the concept of coherent thought is understood. Even once critical thinking develops, we require the intent of a warrior to change established beliefs and fixed neural pathways. By the time our level of maturity and consciousness develops enough that we are able to ask these questions, the patterns are so established that they operate not only unquestioned but undetected as if they didn't exist.

Early installment and repetition of stories and the synaptic pathways that support them establish what knowledge becomes inculcated as true. Like the key codes of a computer, early stories decide the meaning of every keystroke that follows. Barring an act of grace, unless attitudes, beliefs, and emotional tones are disturbed, or acted on by the force of intent, they will keep repeating and reinforcing. These stories of being include the degree of physical tension one lives in, right down to postures, muscular tonalities, and facial expressions.

Down this path, life defaults to established and habituated synaptic patterns that come to feel familiar, normal, true. Habituated thoughts, feelings, and behaviors mean that we rarely consider what else, if anything, might be possible. Beliefs and postures, attitudes, and tonalities, when accepted without question, live beyond conscious perception, and as such discredit, ignore, and generally remain unaffected by contradictory information. When set early and given sufficient repetition, established synaptic pathways become truer by the day. They "just feel right," whether they are or not.

Both the emergence of creativity as well as the habit of defaulting to established behavior exist in the field of potential. Stories enable a process of re-creating experience, which can either function as a source of power in the creation of stories that serve, or cause us to default to the unquestioned repetition of established patterns regardless of their value or efficacy. Life either develops creativity or operates by habit, depending on intent's alignment in the realm of the spirit.

Experience—everything seen and felt, and how the world "seems"— emanates from a relative position, location, quality, or focus of attention. The quality or location of one's attention is the foundation on which the quality of one's life experience is built. Attention's dynamic relationship to experience influences the formation of both thought and life. The ability to position the focus of attention is a fundamental meta-skill, influencing one's state of presence.

When creativity emerges, it matches the level and quality of our consciousness functioning, which changes moment to moment and day to day. The quality of creativity can only be affected from a state of consciousness aware of creative possibility. Even then, knowledge is power only when activated. Otherwise, one lives as the world prevalently lives, according to the effects of established patterns.

Monasteries, ashrams, temples, dojos, and esoteric schools all train their students, at some level, in the skills that give birth to the power of creativity. A tremendous focus of human consciousness has been figuring out what to do to achieve this power. Schools of art and business, as well as sales, marketing, and all forms of propaganda and mind manipulation look at limited aspects of this larger study. Each looks through a certain window and develops a partial description.

As the world, moving from village to country, nation to globe, recognizes itself as one system, ecologically, commercially, politically, and evolutionarily, belief systems based on a single window become less useful. A holographic understanding assembles and develops, changing the story that serves as a basis for operation. This exploration, guided by the leading edge of those who study consciousness, seems to be permeating into the mainstream as human consciousness becomes increasingly aware of the interconnectedness of life.

In the night sky in the desert, where there is no ambient light, the stars come forth at a level of visibility never seen in the city. Similarly, opening to the universal energy in a positive spirit brings forth a field of consciousness that is less obscured. An infinite field of possibilities appears that we never realized existed there. The sky not has changed. Rather, the drive to the desert changes the location of attention. In the realm of the spirit, a dimensional shift in consciousness changes perception of what is so. While under such circumstances we experience an infinite mystical opening into wonder, we are at the same time undergoing the most mundane physical process involving neurons and synapses, electricity and chemicals, and in the quantum world, intent.

Established patterns, the power of repetition, and the whole synaptic process have a very positive nature in the field of potential. These elements can be used to develop patterns that enhance creativity. The problem comes when habituation forms without consciousness, and lies in how invisible the process becomes. When we are unaware of the patterning, should the power of story lead us down the wrong path, life ends up at the wrong destination. Story makes a good servant and a poor master.

THE FLOATING BRIDGE OF HEAVEN

Life bridges an ever-present dynamic between convention and creativity, orthodoxy and irreverence, composition and improvisation, inertia and growth, reproduction and evolution. Shinto mythology tells of "the floating bridge of heaven"—it invokes a mythic bridge that connects the divine and manifest realms, where the two become one: $1 + 1 = 1$. These dual aspects, like north and south poles in a magnetic field, appear separate and at the same time a unity. Unifying seemingly opposing principles or recognizing and reconciling the underlying unity defines the principle behind the floating bridge of heaven, and the term *Ai*, the first syllable in the word *Aikido*. The sword of the Aiki Kami, the divine spirit of Aikido, was so sharp, the story goes, that it cut things together.

Culture, like the individuals that make it up, "stands on the floating bridge of heaven" when honoring the ways of the ancestors while at the same time courageously exploring the mystery. Harmony exists in a realm where the twin forces are in intentional balance, working together in the same time-space; again, $1 + 1 = 1$.

When the curiosity of life energy and the structures of thought and culture function in balance, stories serve as allegories, usable teachings, allies. An understanding of the relativity of position and perception allows myths and beliefs to guide, align, activate, and complete one's role in and contribution to creation's unfolding. Stories can be maps and aids to create a desired life that expresses and fulfills original self . . . or not.

Opportunity lies in claiming knowledge as power through creating stories that serve a warrior's challenge of actualizing the equation $1 + 1 = 1$. Yin and yang together form the universe as one system, just as male and female combine to make one species. In the realm of the spirit, the equation $1 + 1 = 1$ represents thinking and feeling, mind and body, attention and experience—all the various manifestations of yin and yang functioning harmoniously as one system, a unified field.

The unified field of breathing in and breathing out produces and sustains aliveness, just as night and day merge one into the other in the eternal flow of time-space. Creativity is either birthed out of the love that arises when yin and yang complete each other in harmonious relationship . . . or the known continues to repeat itself.

The calling that draws the attention of spirit, the reason why anyone would go to a church, laboratory, dojo, or ashram, is the search for a path that brings the power of habit and the magic of creativity, the manifest and the divine together into a unified field that functions to create a beautiful world. In the song of the winds swirling on the threshold of the unknown, inquiry invites knowledge to dance.

ILLUMINATING THE PATH

With or without conscious attention, for better or for worse, creativity and imagination face life's gift of unfolding challenge. A skill that can be developed, the power of intent, moves attention from habituation and default mode behavior into activating creativity. A finer field of potential interconnection permeates being, both energetically in imagination and also viscerally at the somatic level.

Appreciating and exploring the effect of relativity on perception gradually dissolves the border divorcing the known from the unknown and the established from the innovative. The two positions are not in opposition. They complete and fulfill each other. Developing a relationship of harmony with existence allows communication and becoming one—one understanding, one feeling, one being.

Creativity both initiates and inexorably emerges as the manifestation of the union. Every release of knowing into a spirit permeable to new information potentially increases the innovation of synaptic connections. When we enter experience as a field of inquiry, we open access to, and power to influence and design, the evolving structures of thought and belief.

By positioning the location of feeling in a spirit of sincerity, interest, inquiry, and love, we can listen, understand, and harmonize with the guidance and the energy that creativity offers. Once this energy is activated, it opens the doorway to the unknown, the realm of creativity. The mystery of this realm is not a problem to be solved. It is not something to be avoided or defeated. It is something to be honored, explored, and experienced as one is drawn to the mystery of a lover. The mystery of creation is, above all, to be shown deep respect and loved as sacred. Respect means to look again. In the quantum world, that respect echoes universally, again and again.

Repetitive patterns form habits, potentially by intent or design, but rather more commonly by default. Unless an act of intent or providence intervenes, neural pathways repeat thoughts, feelings, and behaviors the same way they were first formed. Without sufficient "free energy," we default to established synaptic pathways, a pattern that shows up reflexively, physiologically, inevitably. Creating new neural pathways takes significantly more energy, and exponentially more micro-volts, than continuing to habituate down established pathways and patterns of neural energy, thinking, and emotions.

When we lack the necessary free energy to generate new synaptic connections, which includes the knowledge, courage, and intent to use it, neural energy flows along the path of least resistance into established synaptic patterns. Emotional patterns, stories, and systems of thought repeat and fixate as if they make up the only reality. The bucket of life is filled by drops of attention. Our relationships to each pulse of energy, which individually seem so innocuous, cumulatively decide whether the creative process leads toward a joyful and fulfilling life or down less desirable pathways.

Conscious creativity denotes the power to innovate efficient and effective responses to the challenges faced in an infinite, expanding, and evolving universe. It is the power of conscious creativity that has taken humanity from living in the dark, to the mystery manifesting the technological wonders of modern existence and the terrifying, destructive power of modern warfare. The most prevalent stories caused the acceleration of technology. The road less traveled in the realm of the spirit forms a trail toward developing the quality of conscious beings who employ the technology. Tremendous scientific advancement begs for the inspired development of consciousness and spirit, humanity's higher angels.

ENERGY BEINGS IN AN ENERGY UNIVERSE

The process of creativity, while mysterious, isn't really all that mystical. At least in part, it is visceral, physiological chemistry and neurological currents. Creativity requires energy. The Japanese kanji or ideograph *Ki*, the second syllable in Aikido that is often translated as "energy," carries a richer meaning. Ki symbolizes the force of creativity activating and sustaining creation, a force of infinite potential power.

Aikido, commonly translated as "the way of harmony with the energy of the universe," comes out of Japanese martial arts tradition and is a modern expression of an ancient study of energy, the universe, and the source of creation. The founder Morihei Ueshiba, called Osensei, meaning "great teacher" or "teacher's teacher," died in 1969.

Martial arts refers to studies in the realm of Mars, the god of war. Though known in the world primarily for its development of techniques in the martial arts, Aikido also develops harmonious spirit as the basis for creativity in every field and domain, every aspect of life. The principles apply across the spectrum, offering the power of harmony. The founder described the way of the warrior as "the life of loving protection, the source of the activities of science."

In its original usage, Ki symbolizes steam, implying potential power from the Latin verb *poder*, which means "to be able." Power implies ability, possibility, capability, and the energy to create and adapt to change—in other words, creativity. Steam as the union of fire and water metaphorically represents the creative power of the duality of forces that unify $1 + 1 = 1$, activating the creation of time, space, and the universe.

In the mystical, mythical philosophy of the Orient, water seeps downward. Fire burns upward. Together they create steam, or Ki. In a simplistic description, the upward-rising force expresses contribution to the world. The downward-sinking force returns attention to ground, from whence life draws the energy sourcing all power and action. In the rush of energy that occurs in response to any stimulus, a process involving multiple factors determines how we position the focus of attention. The relationship of attention and experience casts one's state of being, the spirit with which one enters life, the foundational quality in the formation of life experience.

Everything affects everything. In reciprocating echoes that emanate out of inner harmony, peace is created in the world of an individual. The echoes of this reciprocation ripple outward, as an individual is part of a family, part of a society, part of humanity, and part of creation. The art of peace harmonizes essence, the central core of self that is propelled on its path to completion via the greater circle: the subtle forces, skills, and effective interactions, and the contributions we make in the world.

Creative beauty flows into the world through the balance between the two, center and circle. Conversely, inner conflict produces destructive Ki. Focusing attention on feeling experience, we move the quality of Ki along the continuum toward beneficial creativity. Every pulse of universal energy, every breath every moment, exists as a field of potential. Conscious choice or the absence thereof either produces harmonious relationship with Ki or causes us to default to reactive behavior, respectively; thus the *potential* of creativity, when misaligned, can cause bad feelings and destructive ends.

In the human domain, the mysterious, vital life force of Ki permeates being, thereby activating experience. As with prana in Sanskrit, chi in Chinese, and élan vital in Western terminology, Ki, at the level of the individual, implies essential personal power, the activating vitality of the central core of being. The concept alludes to the unnamable, indescribable vital force, the impulse of life—the expression of universal creativity through an individual. Ki creates, connects, and activates synaptic pathways that create thoughts, feelings, and the neuromuscular function that activates kinesthetic action in the world.

Action takes place because a signal of intent sent from the brain as neural energy along neural pathways stimulates muscular contraction, the source of kinesthetic motion. The subtle source of intent is a deeper aspect of study. On the threshold of the conscious realm, impulses from the brain express the force of intent that is birthed out of the mystery. As intent forms, expressing the energy dance, the body moves in response. Aikido's harmony arises with the source of energy that motivates action, the original source preceding neural energy, muscular response, and kinesthetic action. Aikido functions in the domain of intent. Intent is the essence of life; and as in every type of study, the deeper the exploration, the greater the mystery.

Ki flows, guiding and guided by intent, which operates in a reciprocating cycle with the focus, quality, or location of attention. Ki implies a quality of spirit. Somewhat honoring the Japanese idiom of "say one word, hear ten words," Ki being originally represented by the pictograph or idiogram for steam or energy also implies the following aspects: common sense, mind, soul, heart, intention, bent, interest, mood, feeling, temper, disposition, nature, attention, air, atmosphere, flavor, and essence.

A practitioner skilled in Eastern medicine, viewing illness as a weakening of Ki, can diagnose health issues by sensing the flow of Ki in a person's energy field. Acupuncture and shiatsu massage are forms of healing that focus on stimulating the flow of Ki through the meridians, the channels that conduct Ki to and through the physical body in the manifest realm.

Energy is intelligence. Within the energy that sustains creation are glimmers of an amazing intelligence, enough intelligence to keep the planets spinning in their orbits, enough intelligence to circulate the blood of infinite creatures. The intelligence at play in a human system keeps all the bio-electrochemical interactions going on; it is an incredible intelligence. The word *Ki* implies all that.

THE RUSH

In response to any stimulus, change, challenge, job, or situation, an increasing flow, a rush of energy floods the system to enhance ability.

The quantity and quality of Ki influence the power to handle change. Ki is magnetized into the radiance of the alive system at a level of intensity that matches the perceived need, challenge, or job, thus helping to bring it to successful completion.

Aliveness manifests through and from unformed potential, energy, power, and possibility. Energy, when skillfully channeled, produces effectiveness. Though positive in its original intent, the rush of Ki can produce positive or negative effects depending on the quality of the relationship that exists between attention and the experience of "reactivity," an energetic, surging, bio-electromagnetic vitality.

We possess reserves of energy beyond normal levels, which are critical to our survival, offering safety and protection, allowing us to run away from danger or handle a challenge—anything it takes for success in satisfactorily negotiating life. When those reserves are tapped in an emergency, tremendous amounts of energy become available. As the energy increases, so does what is possible. With increased power comes increased responsibility; attention must equally balance our stance on the bridge between center and circle, linking the central core and the world of subtle force(s).

Ki flows into reactivity, or energy on the move. The surging energy or energy rush is felt first as pressure on the system. This rush is triggered in response to any stimulus, whether a challenge of life and death or something as innocuous as ascertaining the time. When we feel threatened, there can be a huge rush of energy emanating through the core of being, which overrides conscious process. We react visibly when startled. The startle response is an example of a reaction to a too-much, too-fast rush of energy.

Though typically only noticed when a reaction reaches sufficient intensity, the process occurs at lower levels relative to every stimulus, startlement, surprise, or situation. The size of the wave rushing through the system and the intensity of its effect vary depending on the situation. However, the fundamentals remain the same.

The movement of physical energy—muscle tension, hormones, breathing—and mental-emotional energy—the flood of thoughts and feelings, the startle reaction—are the result of the subtle energy of Ki.

Reactivity, a system's activation in response to increased Ki, shows up as a feeling of change, a flow, an increase in energy, a charge, a whispering of a mystical echo, a disturbance in the force. The shift in Ki flow can happen in response to any change, need, or challenge, whether from exhaustion, religious ritual, or seemingly inexplicably. The flow is always shifting at some level, and these shifts can either be subtle and go unnoticed or they can be intense, going from startling to traumatic.

As the system greets energy, it generates a tonality, a field of potential. Resonant neural pathways form, reinforcing any propensity that is established. The quality and tonality of the system's relationship with energy sets up the spirit with which one enters the world.

Warrior training intentionally utilizes the energetic rush, channeling energy, amplifying the call to effective action in the face of change. The challenge, the art, and the dance all set the foundation on which the quality of every thought and action is built, and stay in harmonious relationship with the rush of vitality, making one "comfortable"—in possession of able power. Aiki, responding harmoniously to the unfolding of the universe, allows Ki to express its natural creativity.

Mastery practices develop focus and proficiency in the art of moving one's attention in creative response to an ever-changing universe. Aikido teaches and practices entering life in a fluid spirit of adaptability, whether the moment appears life threatening or seemingly insignificant. The story of Aiki promotes the life choice to intentionally, attentively, and experientially harmonize with the creative source.

PRECISION FOCUS

All the aspects of being come together to form an interconnected, interdependent system. Everything affects everything. When we activate a specific muscle or muscle group, every muscle in the body tends to tighten in resonance. Any unneeded tension drains energy, weakening signal transmission. At the same time, resistance impedes speed, power, and range of motion in the physical sphere, and equally in the realm of thought and affect or feeling. Releasing unneeded "sympathetic" tension frees energy, empowering us toward desired action. Free energy returns to source, becoming available to create new synaptic connections and utilize established connections more effectively.

Mastery, in the realm of physical movement, implies the ability to activate specific muscles required for an action, while relaxing all the rest at the same time. A master's focus frees them to engage in energy channeling and presence, utilizing countless microvolts of bio-electromagnetic aliveness previously spent in resistance. The master can instead put these microvolts into the intended action, thus increasing the creativity of thought and the speed, power, and precision in the execution of any movement.

The same principle—unifying precision, in the focus, and relaxation—at the same time produces mastery in every realm, including the manifest, hidden, and divine; and in every domain, comprising body, mind, and spirit. Relaxation, whether of our muscles or opinions, and the act of simply feeling, centering, and grounding, radiates on all levels, releasing tension into flow. Free energy generates power, producing feelings of security and confidence that reinforce relaxation, leading to openness, creativity, and enjoyment of experience.

In the right alignment and at the appropriate level of intensity, a rush of energy is something people love, enjoy, and seek. Falling in love is one of the defining energy rushes in human experience. Similarly, the hormonal-chemical release of an adrenaline rush is virtually addictive for people who "love" to play sports, or music, or who love to travel to new places or climb mountains. Positive Ki, entering into and unifying with the energy of experience in a positive spirit, evokes joy.

Extreme sports are an extreme version of this rush. That is, they promote a harmonious relationship to, and therefore a positive experience with, the energy rush. The challenge involved is fun. It is sought. That's why people do extreme sports, races, and dangerous things: because life loves the rush of life, of vitality, which is energy. The ability to function in the physical brings attention into the physical, into the moment. Danger increases energy and presence, which, when they are in harmonious relationship, can be exhilarating. Too little or too much energy for one's level of presence, however, and it is a different story.

To be aligned in positive, harmonious relationship with Ki, a state of being sometimes called the flow state, can be the best experience one can have, and is what is addictive about the aforementioned activities. Ki, when it is right, defines joy and potentially a lot more—the peak experiences of life.

The energy rush adjusts in response to the organism's perceived need. In the face of any stimulus—a memory, red lights flashing in a rearview mirror, trying to remember what to buy at the store, missing the bus, or, dramatically, in the face of a violent physical attack—a rush of energy hits the system viscerally. An emergency calls up a big rush of energy. A smaller challenge calls up a smaller rush of energy. The more critical the outcome of a challenge, the bigger the rush of energy.

A strong enough rush overloading the system, impeding its ability to function, comes to be described as terror. As more energy produces increased reactivity, attention to center becomes increasingly important in equal proportion. Harmonizing with the rush of energy activated by change is the practice and process of Aiki.

The energy rush is evolutionarily driven to increase our effectiveness, but too much too fast and the system can't process it. When the rush overwhelms, that is a bifurcation point. It happens quickly and generally passes unnoticed. Resisting the energy will point us down the road to fear, which leads to anger and aggression.

We become "out of sorts" when the alignment is off and the energy rush is disturbing enough, and under such circumstances, reactivity—implying reaction before conscious process—attacks, avoids, shuts down, fights, flees, or freezes. Given the right ingredients, or a sufficient level of intensity, the subconscious turns the rush into monsters in dreams or imagination. This occurs in proportion to the intensity of the rush and the degree of misalignment or resistance.

Training channels energy to a first response that recognizes reactivity and effectively processes it. When we move our point of focus, the location of attention transforms reactivity into a harmonious spirit, and the alive system intrinsically rediscovers its self as dynamic energy, creativity, ongoing growth, and development.

Life experience pivots on the location of the focus of attention, whether positioned consciously or by default. The spiritual quest, the journey of the spirit, is a way of intentionally moving the location of the glow of attention, positioning it to allow us to feel better, meaning both heightened sensory acuity and more enjoyable internal alignment.

The positioning of attention is a mysterious factor in why experience is so mutable. In brain pattern activity, specific areas of the brain light up in differing degrees at different times. All neural reactivity interacts with intent and attention, relative to different moods and other known as well as yet-unknown variables. Whether intentionally activating the state of feeling better, or surrendering thought and affect to habituated attitudes, the smallest degree of change in course affects the passage and destination of life's journey.

WHOLE-BRAIN THINKING

The messages of the varying aspects of being often conflict, causing moments of confusion and indecision as the varying aspects of neural processing collate perception and strategy. Life energy, when properly aligned, activates and balances the higher cortical functions of the tri-une brain. Balanced communication between the functions allows the cerebrum and frontal lobes to receive, harmonize, and utilize information from the lower systems rather than being left behind in the process or left out altogether.

Unless it is grounded, reactivity, expressing ancient neural patterns, tends to operate out of a binary lack of creativity. When functioning under the organizing magnetic influence of the higher cortical aspects of cognitive power, the same energy, as it becomes coherent, produces laser-like thinking, cutting through problems and producing precision action for greater effect with less effort.

The study of Aikido develops a unified field of whole-brain thinking where all the aspects unify holistically, magnifying effectiveness. The superpower coming out of holistic perception, distilled from whole-brain processing, empowers the improvisational magic of spontaneous creativity, generating new learning in the moment.

The stages of brain development in the medulla, cerebellum, cerebrum, and frontal lobes, as well as the left and right hemispheres of the brain, send multiple and conflicting messages, each in their own language. Physiologically, intelligence develops from perception, which includes and unifies input from multiple aspects of the brain.

In the present story, a field of intelligence emerges from the unification of the two hemispheres of the cerebrum, currently deemed the analytic and the artistic, though incomplete analogues. Communication signals go back and forth through the corpus callosum, giving birth to a holographic comprehension. Two eyes produce depth of field and two sexes give birth to one species. The hemispheres interconnect, functioning as one system to produce enhanced intelligence, $1 + 1 = 1$.

The basal ganglia and the thalamic and cerebral systems are involved in distinct roles and temporal dynamics of neural processing, reflecting their specialized functions within the brain. They function, in effect, with different time frames, at different clock speeds, and in different languages. Consciousness mediates the mixed messages coming from the varying levels of brain development. In response to a high-pressure situation, data volume can overload the information processing capability of the system, pushing it toward default behavior. Tension drains potential creativity.

Aikido, through the principle of unification, activates responses through the whole system of intelligence. The power of unification peacefully reconciles conflicts that the aspects of cognition may have with one another's perceptions and processes. Harmony transforms resistance into the power of unformed potential. Free energy unifies a creative whole-brain response in a positive, reinforcing cycle.

Thesis, antithesis, synthesis: when a force and its counterpart unify, the synthesis creates a new domain of possibility. When right brain and left brain function as one system, a holistic, increasingly coherent intelligence appears. In a similar way, new life is created out of unification of male and female; no amount of either alone has that ability. Creation is the outcome of unification, just as water is born from the union of hydrogen and oxygen. These elements are all the same thing, and yet not, as the cutting edge of a sword is both sides of the blade and/or neither. The story depends on point of view and the process of making meaning, and at best captures only a fraction of the totality of WIGO.

Harmonizing into unification with the movement of an attack diffuses force or impact. Unifying with internal energy movement diffuses the pressure to react before fully processing an issue. Unifying the inner field of being produces a resonant unification with the world at large. By moving with the energy of change or pressure in any situation, Aikido transforms force into a field of potential, opening possibilities of peaceful resolution where none existed. Generating life from a spirit of harmony gives birth to flexibility and responsiveness. The concept of "never defeated means never fighting" implies infinite, spontaneous creativity.

In its physical application, Aikido technique joins with the energy of an attack "a second before," when it is still forming in the attacker's mind. Aikido happens before the neural signals ever reach the musculature, before kinesthetic action begins. Aikido's influence on attention lives at the point where experience turns into meaning. As feeling turns into thought in the hidden realms, Aiki blends the two, influencing power before it forms in the manifest realm, before it becomes action or words.

PRESENCE AND HARMONY

The power of presence produces whole-brain thinking. Including the corpus, the soma, and the harmony produces whole-being presence, the unified field experience. The intelligence of the universe flows into the world through the union of the total alive system, which encompasses the mind-body-spirit, the left brain and right brain, and the thalamic, cortical, cerebral, neurological, muscular, breathing, thinking, feeling, sensing, and knowing systems.

Psyche, soma, and corpus, identified and named as separate aspects for conversation and study, represent an indivisible, interdependent system, all aspects together co-creating the whole. The term *soma* in the Greek terminology relates to the realm of feeling and sensory perception. Somatic sensing means feeling or experiencing something beyond explanation. The implications of soma—"sensing, feeling, knowing"—spill over into what might be described by the word *mind*.

Psyche, from the Greek *psyche*, has been defined as "the soul, mind, spirit, or invisible animating entity which occupies the physical body." A loose translation of the word *psyche* includes both thought and emotion. Definitions of the words *mind* and *spirit* interpenetrate, yet spirit extends and activates beyond the realm *mind* describes. None of the three—psyche, soma, or corpus—encompass in their modern usage the quantum inferences of the word *spirit*. As the activating, interpenetrating, universal force of being, spirit permeates the entire field of every aspect in the hidden and manifest realms.

Spiritual practice can be accessed through any of the realms or domains, as they are all interconnected. Just as stretching increases the body's flexibility, and with it range of motion, stretching the mind opens the door to new synaptic connections and creative thinking. Stretching emotionally can increase emotional intelligence, or "feeling better," which in turn enhances somatic connection with the universe. They all influence each other. In every dimension, exercises that increase "range of motion" enhance the ability of the system to spontaneously, creatively respond in harmony with the mysterious, universal unfolding.

THE THALAMIC PAUSE:
STOP AND THINK ABOUT IT

The Thalamic Pause, a concept aligned with Alfred Korzybski's principles of pausing to avoid automatic responses, represents time to allow thought to move from the reptilian brain's first reaction, allowing it to include and integrate the limbic and higher cortical function, producing a unified field of "whole-brain thinking." The Thalamic Pause, sometimes called the semantic pause, empowers the movement from reaction to response.

Shining the light of attention on propensities of neural processing opens the possibility of moving beyond autonomic functioning and instinctual or habitual behaviors, from reptilian to mammalian to human, reactive to impulsive to deliberative. Given time and intent, the three brains and the left and right hemispheres can have a conversation, and working together they produce a coherent whole-brain understanding. It is a process. It gets faster with practice.

Harmonizing attention and experience frees energy to express its inherent nature as creativity. New synaptic connections come into being due to the increased availability of energy. Turning up the rheostat of consciousness charges the field of potential. The essential joy emanating from the essence of being naturally supplying energy from the source of creation. As one assimilates spiritual nourishment, awareness glows with vitality in response, engendering a quantum leap in imagination and creative flow.

A centered, grounded, unified field creates choice, power, and possibility. Increased potential empowers us to enter into the unknown with a positive spirit, with confidence, like going to the market with more than enough money. What is impossible at one level of free energy becomes possible at another.

Presence, cultivating a spirit of harmony with the universe as it unfolds, leads beyond habits, outmoded thought, and outdated understanding. Freeing the energy that is necessary to create new synaptic connections allows us to respond to each experience anew. When we locate attention in a spirit of harmony, this informs outcomes that are creatively adapted and appropriate to each unique situation through time-space. That is what harmony means.

Centering and grounding activates a state that frees energy otherwise drained into tension. Presence channels energy via intent. In life, presence means locating attention in the driver's seat. The process of presence—how to get here, where *here* is, and exactly who or what is becoming present—has been the topic of stories since they began.

ALIGNING PRESENCE

Stories condense knowledge, making it easier to figure out what to do. Stories come and go, and there is no way to predict what the next one will be. Many stories exist at the same time with varying degrees of popularity. Differing stories vie for dominance in a competition between ideas that drive society, as well as between the aspects within an individual. As one part of the complexity that feeds energy to the conflict, increasing polarization reinforces a primitive, binary mind-set of right and wrong. The reptilian brain reacts quickly on a narrow eat-or-be-eaten spectrum.

In defensive mode, attention moves in the opposite direction from the location or quality that produces creativity. As a discussion heats up, rising temperatures push attention toward talking and away from listening. As always, the same process is reverberating internally, between attention and experience, blocking listening internally and externally at the same time. The intensity of the reptilian brain's high-speed survival response of fear and aggression, which evolved early in our evolutionary development, too often overrides the slower, quieter deliberative cortical function, hijacking any possibility of thoughtful dialogue and collaborative resolution.

History has been a catalogue of Shakespearean tragedy filled with missed messages, misunderstood communications, and the ensuing conflicts of war, oppression, and brutality. All too often, petty misunderstandings destroy the delicate trust needed to allow cooperation between individuals and between nations. Distrust incubates fear, and in that story, creativity pursues outcomes of destruction.

We fight too many wars, personal and international; so much of human conflict emanates out of emotionally triggered reactivity as the seed crystal of interaction, rather than incorporating the guidance of reason to produce a better outcome. Suffering then ensues from conflict that arises from misconstrued, misrepresented, and misunderstood stories that potentially in a quantum world could have been told differently, leading to an amicable resolution. There may be things worth dying for. Misunderstanding, especially misunderstanding that could have been resolved, is not the intelligent option.

That is the story coming out of brain development. Every step down the path of enmity requires many times that number of steps in the reverse direction to recover trust. Trust, to whatever degree it exists, is the seed crystal in the formation of the quality of every human interaction, internal and external. An argument, which can go so wrong so quickly, can turn into a loving relationship with a kind word. The spirit of reconciliation can transform the tension of a moment, creating completely different outcomes.

In a potential field of trust, what stories could learn from each other and produce together is unimaginable. When we feel as both an individual part of humanity and at the same time as part of a larger process of "truth," it becomes possible to triangulate perception among multiple points of observation. The possibilities synergy opens are as infinite as they are unpredictable.

When the system is activated as a unified field, whole-brain thinking resolves what first appears as dissonance, transforming it into confluence. The reciprocating echoes start internally and engage the universe. The process of meaningful dialogue, through intentionally balancing the upward-rising with the downward-sinking forces, attracts the creative voice of inner wisdom, which speaks in a language of peaceful reconciliation. This dynamic is equally true and valuable within and between individuals, cultures, and nations.

2

QUANTUM UNDERSTANDING

The value of collaboration in the story of the development of human knowledge is incalculable. Producing an increasingly holistic model offers an enlightened viewpoint from which to predict future possibilities and to develop future strategies. When we synergize differing views, myriad options for inquiry, dialogue, and creative resolution appear that don't exist in a world of fixed positions, similar to the increased creative options produced by mixing primary colors.

When the regions of the brain operate symphonically, attuned in harmonious relationship, the potential of creating new synaptic connections, new neural pathways, and new possibilities of function magnifies exponentially. Understanding and identifying the bifurcation point where the system is potentially mutable brings the field of potential into conscious attention, enhancing the possibility of volitional influence.

When activated, aligned, and integrated, the unconscious, subconscious, conscious, and superconscious seem to recover their function as a unified field. This function is just a story, but in the field of potential that is produced when the center of attention and the center of the energy core unify experientially, positioning themselves together in time and space, it is as if the system comes out of sleep mode into active function.

Modern science can now track which areas of the brain "light up" in relationship to specific actions and functions. Different physical locations of the brain come out of sleep mode as they activate different life processes. Activating the multiple aspects of the brain, together, at the same time, collates their input. As they synchronize into symphonic resonance, the multiple perspectives integrate into holographic perception, comprehension, and understanding.

Through observation and description, humanity's infinite potential collapses into the mindsets and social systems that direct and bind life. Every interaction and interconnection between forces, people, or aspects within a person exists as a field of unformed potential until it collapses into experience and feeling. When crystallizing into meaning, a story produces either creative or default behavior. The degree to which inner conflict reconciles is the field out of which stories of either confluence or conflict emanate into the world.

A world conscious of the relativity of "truth" deepens the possibility of inquiring together. In a field of potential, a story leading to war could instead be rewritten with a seed crystal of harmony, thus reconciling the world, making human beings one family, and focusing all the power, imagination, and creativity of humanity to create a beautiful world. Though it can occur as an act of grace, most commonly it is an act of intent that brings the thinking, feeling, and creative aspects of being into the unified field experience.

Though the paths up Mount Fuji are infinite in number, the summit is always "one." The peak and purpose of training's first step is always inner harmony, which is a spiritual warrior's primary responsibility. Once experiential alignment is reconciled internally, a spirit of harmony exudes into the world.

Directing attention, and feeling into the central core of one's being, opens a portal to a field of infinite creative energy. The choice to focus attention, to experience feeling as a visceral sensation, dissolves emotional tonality, affect, and identity into the pure, glowing energy of self. From a centered and grounded state of inner harmony, the art of Aikido extends a life of harmony *in and with* the world. And whether or not this story of quantum harmony is truly accurate, it is useful. The proof is in the pudding: the quality of our life experience.

CREATIVITY: SPONTANEOUS INNOVATION

Intentionally enjoying feeling into the aliveness of vitality births infinite spontaneous creativity, and a path surfaces from the face of the unknown. The challenge in a mysterious and changing world lies in focusing creativity on the right goals, with the right intentions, designing the right thing to do, even when the answer only exists as a field of potential. The danger arises should attention, losing its totality, shrink to locate in and operate out of the default mode network, an area of the brain that processes "not knowing what to do."

In present theory the primary functions of a large-scale brain network, termed the default mode network (DMN), include: self-referential thought, memory consolidation, thinking about others, mind-wandering and daydreaming, planning and imagination, and internal mental simulations. When failing to integrate with the whole system, the DMN defaults into processing the unknown as anxiety. Cumulative anxiety flows into a story of fear, with all its repercussions.

In a vicious cycle, when attention loses connection to the somatic aspect—the vibrant, visceral, corporal experience—and moves primarily into the psyche, attention shrinks into rumination and is taken by the default mode network. The related neurological activity can be traced with modern instrumentation. Presence dissolves into projecting concerns about the past or the future. Anxiety or regret claim attention and diminish the sensory power of somatic experience. Physical radiant presence diminishes, activating loss of neurological potential in corresponding measure.

Anxiety and fear, through no fault of their own, end up stealing the energy needed for creativity. Under increased pressure and lacking access to creative energy, the brain's reptilian reactivity sees no other option but to freeze, flee, or turn to aggression. The speed of reaction at the brain stem occurs so quickly that the cerebral process hardly has a chance to intervene.

At rush hour, or whenever we're in a rush, pressure increases due to an increasing flow of information trying to get through a too-small number of functioning neural pathways. That is the moment where *feeling* may be the most undervalued word in the English language. Feeling shifts the location of attention beyond the default mode network, and its potential creativity collapses into the area of the brain that lives in regret and anxiety, activating a larger experiential field of presence. Feeling expands to activate the whole energy processing system.

Simply focusing attention into feeling reverses the process, bringing it out of the default mode network and toward a unified fight flight freeze field experience of whole-being presence. Locating attention into a state of flow in feeling unifies the field of being. The channel of being expands to accommodate the intensity of the rush. Deepening feeling, freeing attention from capture by the default mode network, transforms pressure into the life glow of exalted guidance and isolation within in every dimension, allowing and engaging the unified field of being.

From meditation to basketball, from walks in the woods to skiing black diamond slopes, the activities activating experiential presence awaken and amalgamate the somatic aspect, the power of feeling. These activities increase our "felt sense" according to their degree of intensity. Even the smallest amount of the simplest physical activity points our attention into the experiential realm.

Feeling (i.e. connecting attention with experience) puts the alive system into a state of flow. People with a more internal nature might prefer meditation, weaving, painting, sculpture, music, architecture, mathematics, scientific theory, theoretical science, or contemplative arts. Sitting quietly in meditation or contemplation, focusing attention into the experiential feeling of the breath moving in and out of the lungs, is sufficient to expand the mind, activating a broader area of the brain and a more holistic somatic sense. Precision alignment into the central core, when felt experientially, unifies whole-brain function, whole-being presence, creating the unified field experience.

It doesn't matter "how"; what matters is "that" attention opens into experiential process, distilling a unified field. Anything that causes attention to focus on somatic experience brings the two together in a

$1 + 1 = 1$ process of unification. Through training, the process can be refined and increasingly sophisticated. Either attention positions focus on what is important, or it will be taken by a million incidental distractions.

The power that gives birth to the rush of aliveness potentially startles attention, pushing Ki out of feeling experientially, and instead into stories describing experience. Unpleasant stories especially, but sometimes even pleasant ones, give birth to extensive rumination. Memories from incomplete experience can go back decades and still disturb brain wave patterns, draining upon attention. To feel is to experience the now, as opposed to disassociating, musing, or talking about it, especially to oneself.

Presence, the degree of being here and now, experiencing Ki, sets the tone influencing the quality of every aspect of life. In the quantum world, presence and quality of life are the same thing in mutual creation. When the energy of reactivity surges ungrounded, it leads away from the power of listening. As balance refines between center and circle in each finer dimension, reactivity grounds itself, becoming available as free energy, a willingness and capacity to listen.

Peaceful reconciliation creates a field of acceptance. Peaceful reconciliation melts any fragmented aspect back into the totality. In the quantum world, in the dissolution, nothing is lost. It is rather returned to the field of potential. Releasing dissonance with the past into free energy empowers our entry into the future with no debt and a spiritual bank account overflowing with enthusiasm in the form of creativity.

Life, to a surprising degree, pivots on whatever story we train ourselves to believe via repetition. Activating the whole brain as a unified system creates a different quality of story, taking life on an altogether different journey. The power of harmony transforms the story named *fear* into a call to action in the spirit of the great love of which Aikido's founder spoke.

Aiki is the realization of the oneness of the force of creation and that which it creates. The founder spoke of harmonizing with the movement of the universe, thereby coming into accord with the universal totality.

The unified field, the source of creation in the poetry of the founder, is the one radiant source, "a great love omnipresent in all times and quarters of the universe," and is why he described Aikido as the realization of love.

The radiant gravity of the field unifies the energies, activating all aspects of being. Creativity emanates in resonance. Both Aikido and quantum mechanics offer key codes to translate and comprehend energy's guidance. The power of harmony, Aiki, is the journey of spirit moving into alignment with the intelligence of the energy of creation, absorbing and enjoying its wisdom through life's unfolding.

ENERGY IS FORM AND FORM IS ENERGY

The insights of modern physics, relativity, and quantum mechanics describe matter as energy, and the field of "both/and" has changed the perceptions of science. The concept began to crystallize as a description of an exchange, transformation, or oscillating transition back and forth between energy and matter in units called quanta, and the theory of quantum mechanics was born. In physics, a quantum (plural quanta) is the minimum amount of physical energy involved in an interaction. Quantization of energy and its influence on how energy and matter interact is part of the fundamental framework for understanding the prevalent story describing nature.

The term *quantum leap*, originally describing an abrupt transition from one energy state to another, has come to be used figuratively to describe a sudden large advance, an extraordinary movement forward in knowledge or capability. Subatomic particles, for example, were a dramatic breakthrough from the accepted science of atoms as solid matter. It was a quantum leap to imagine subatomic particles seemingly appearing out of an interpenetrating flow or interconnecting dimensional link between energy and matter. As the indivisibility of the atom proved to be an illusion, so may the distinction of the quantum as science continues to progress. The beauty lies less in the knowing and more in the exploration of the mystery.

Energy is vibration, a back-and-forth, plus-and-minus, on-and-off duality that makes up a unity of $1 + 1 = 1$. Everything is vibration. Subatomic particles seem to be more of a process, rapidly shifting back and forth between appearing as form and dissolving into a field of unformed potential. Back-and-forth creates everything, except perhaps that which precedes and/or creates back-and-forth, a force that, akin to the mind of God, is presently unknown, and possibly unknowable.

Energy as vibration pulsates, surging and receding in waves, building to a peak, transitioning to the opposite extreme, and reverting once again: back and forth—yin into yang, day into night. Energy flows in waves and pulses. Each of the waves has a specific frequency and intensity, transacting with, affecting, and being affected by the entire field. The permutations of variations of vibration, the potential possibilities between the ones and zeros, the on-and-off and the back-and-forth, exceed imagination.

When scientists look at light through one experiment, it's a wave. When they look through another, it's a particle. The universe oscillates between dynamic states of emptiness, energy, and static form or, in Aiki terminology, the divine hidden and manifest realms. We see by observation that the field of energy can appear as matter. Unlimited potential can collapse into a specific form. The field of awareness brings the universe into form according to the angle or state of being from which it is observed.

The teachings about Ki from ancient texts teach principles aligned with the discoveries of modern physics. When science was in its infancy, the Greeks postulated the atom, an innovative idea at the time. Long before the energy equations of modern physics, the ancient systems taught that "form is emptiness and emptiness is form."

In Hindu mythology, the dance of Shiva sustains all creation. Only so long as Shiva is dancing does the world continue to evolve and change. Whenever Shiva stops dancing, the world collapses back into nothingness, no-thing-ness, energy. Absent the observer, so does wave particle duality.

In one version of the present story, subatomic particles form out of energy and dissolve back into unformed potential rapidly, creating the illusion of solid matter. In another view, both formation and dissolution are happening at the same time, in the same time-space. A story appears out of the world of modern physics to describe something incomprehensible. There are no "things." Every*thing* is mutable. Every "thing" is energy; in fact, *thing* is the wrong word. Whatever goes back and forth as energy will form, or change, every*thing*. The true breakthrough of modern physics might be translated as "no thing is solid"; or rather, it is and it isn't.

Science, moving from seeing time and space as two separate things, now uses the term time-space. Scientific understanding has shifted from seeing energy and matter as two separate things, to seeing an experience no one understands; and if no one understands, how could they possibly describe it? Yet when interacting to collect the intelligence of a larger field, scientists talk to one another about it. As a result, they end up creating descriptions that contain more approximation than precision.

The forces of the universe show up in polarity: yin-yang, light-dark, male-female, the artistic and analytic sides of nature, matter-spirit/energy, thought-action, and known-unknown. Each polarity is inseparable from the other, and from the dynamic, just as left and right, front and back, and top and bottom are unified in any three-dimensional object.

Energy and matter are two states of one domain beyond present comprehension. In the world of duality, opposites are seen in opposition. In the Aiki-land of the unified field, polarities, when observed, are seen as aspects of a field that magnetizes out of the radiance of creativity. When the aspects of mind/body, left brain / right brain, conscious/unconscious, or masculine/feminine connect and balance, the field functions optimally, enjoying itself and doing what it does best as an interpenetrating part of a cosmic unfolding.

The unified field sources the creation of the polarities and vice versa, just as improvisation and composition unify in a field of music. Whether we are using our lungs to breathe in or breathe out at any given moment, the two actions occur within one system. The magic of Aiki cuts things together: one plus one equals one. Unification creates and sustains everything in life experience.

THE ENERGY FIELD: POTENTIAL AND CREATION

The universe of galaxies is mostly empty space. Galaxies are mostly empty space. Solar systems are mostly empty space. That is how atoms are: way more emptiness and nothingness than matter. Solid matter is mostly space between subatomic particles that don't exactly exist either. These entities seem to be energy fields more than solid particles, yet once observed, they behave like particles. Attempting to describe any of this is nearly futile—as if linear words could describe an unfathomable process, especially since that being described is more unknown than known.

Creation seems to flash back and forth from energy into form, forming and dissolving at the same time. A field of energy in transformation is perceived as solid matter, like moving images on a screen that appear as a movie. It's an illusion, a flickering lamp, a phantom, and a dream.

The technical forms in Aikido are shown to open the doorway for the student to step into the realm of infinite, spontaneous creativity. The founder spoke of the absence of form in Aikido, describing the appearance of forms and techniques as "the dust after the action." Energy follows attention from dissonance toward harmony. Of course, forms appear and dissolve in the manifest realm, but they are the effect of the process, not the process itself. Aikido is what takes place within the energy of an attack, in the hidden realms of energy and divine realms of creativity, in the moment when the attack is still forming.

In an interesting turn of events, the scientific experiment that was conducted to clarify and resolve curiosity about matter and energy brought a new element into the equations. In the realm of quantum entanglement, in the now-famous wave-particle double slit experiment, scientists, in attempting to determine whether light was a wave or a particle, projected light through one slit. It appeared to show up as a particle, but then they did the same experiment shining the light through a double slit, and it showed itself as a wave. This led the scientific community to recognize that light was either energy and/or matter, depending on how one looked at it or set up the experiment. From a larger perspective, they are one system. How the experiment is set up changes experience, or in this case changes reality. The experiment has led some scientists to speculate that consciousness could be influencing reality. Scientists performing the experiment found that *how* they looked at its results altered what they saw. When this possibility surfaced, it caused a dramatic shift. Prior to that illumination, science either seemingly preferred or had simply habituated to a story that left consciousness out of the world of objective scientific experiment.

As the idea that consciousness permeates and affects creation seeps into our consciousness, at the same time, the meaning of *consciousness* eludes present definition. Opinions differ. Dictionaries talk circles around the meaning in words that substitute but don't define. Medical science talks about what consciousness *does*. What it *is* seems presently beyond human understanding, making our descriptions the product of human innovation. For the present, what exactly consciousness means falls under the uncertainty principle. Consciousness, without knowing itself what it is, exists as an idea in a field of potential possibility, which collapses into understanding in the mind of the translator.

Classical science prefers the story of impartial observation in large part due to the inability to measure subjective reality. Impartial observation implies observation in a universe in which the observer does not exist. Yet by definition, nothing in the universe exists independent of the universe. The impartial observation story of classical science doesn't really work in the quantum world. In an energy universe, there's no way to separate anything out from affecting everything else.

An aspect that resonated with the concept of consciousness was present in the Newtonian equation. This aspect was thought of as divine power and seen as an outside force. One key distinction between the quantum and classical views was that Newton believed in God as the watchmaker of the universal machine, separate from his creation. Newton's thought functioned within the limits of the prevailing paradigm of his era, with sovereigns and rulers separate from and controlling the people they governed. Because that was the world he lived in, he saw people as subjects of, rather than members of and participants in, the divine force of creation.

The quantum insight about the observer affecting the experiment indicates a shift away from Newton's view. Newton saw a cold, mechanical universe run by a separate watchmaker. Quantum mechanics tells the story of an interrelationship between matter, energy, and consciousness, a unified field theory of an incomprehensible and ever-changing universal flux. All this is a mystery so vast it cannot be spoken; and yet at the same time, it simply *is*.

THE ILLUSION OF CENTRAL POSITION: CREATION MYTHS AND BEYOND

In the search for the origin of creation and the meaning of self, belief systems of many kinds have produced enchanting stories explaining where the universe comes from and how it works, and prescribing a course of action to work with it. A culture's guidance is coded in its creation myths, rites, and religious rituals. As numerous and creative as the cultures and individuals that give birth to them, these stories, absorbed from clan and culture as archetypes, influence the unique, imaginary stories that create an individual's world. Most ancient cultures have a creation myth. So do most modern cultures and most religions. And so does science.

Stories, a bit like fingerprints, have a lot of similarities to one another, but each individual creates a unique version. Similar stories develop different meanings based on the understanding of the individual creating their own interpretation through a unique synaptic network. Everyone interprets their own understanding of existing stories on top of inevitably creating endless stories of their own. The creation of story is an autonomic process that simply happens. The human brain creates meaning just as a plant gives off oxygen, or an animal releases carbon dioxide. In the natural course of life, stories are birthed as if they came out of nowhere. Through focusing attention, one can see the process of creativity unfold. Engaging attention in the creative process is what turns life into art.

Story as artistic creativity doesn't have to be accurate or true. Synaptic patterns don't have to make sense for the mind to connect them. Commonly, story creates an evolving illusion of how things are, based on a limited perception of how they look at a specific point in time-space, overlaid with meaning from experience and stories past, and infused with ample quantities and qualities of the magic of imagination, or creativity.

Prior to the Renaissance, cosmological folklore around the globe was influenced by a syndrome that psychology labels "the illusion of central position." This describes the initial perception from an infant's relative vantage point that the universe revolves around the infant. In an adult, the illusion of central position carries over, showing up as the virtually unquestioned assumption that the beliefs one holds are central and correct.

The illusion of central position gave birth to a geocentric view of the cosmos. This story describes Earth as the stable center around which the universe revolves. One myth tells of a flat Earth resting on the back of an elephant that stands on the back of a turtle. Famously, when philosopher and psychologist William James challenged a believer asking what the turtle stands on, she responded, "It's no use, Mr. James. It's turtles all the way down."

Based on present science, it may seem hard to imagine that people really believed this was actual and not mythic, symbolic, or metaphoric. Yet it exemplifies only one of many stories that people once imagined, lived in, and believed, each in their own way—of which many persist to this day. Cultures live in beliefs handed down from earlier stories.

Once adopted, a story doesn't have to make sense for the mind to believe it. Repetition, rather than accuracy, deepens our neural pathways. Once established, a belief doesn't have to make sense for the human mind to defend it. In the clash and confusion of internalized stories with WIGO, early formation and repetition can be a challenge to override.

As the pathways deepen through repetition, confirmation bias sets in. Information that does not fit existing beliefs tends to be discredited and disregarded. Conversely, information that supports established synaptic pathways is treated as highly credible. Following favorite pathways is so easy and feels so right. The hidden dimension, the imprinted system of meaning, remains unseen even as it colors every aspect of thought, feeling, and action. Confirmation bias, cognitive dissonance, as well as the propensity to fit incoming information into existing beliefs, commonly remain invisible to the individual affected.

Greater knowledge alone does not change this propensity. Liberation, seeing beyond thought and belief as systems of repeated patterns, pathways, and neural processes, requires an exceptional focus of immeasurably precious attention. Lack of sufficient energy, whatever the reason, leads to a vicious cycle of resistance to change instead of one of harmonizing with the energy needed for creativity.

To creatively adapt a phrase from the Declaration of Independence: "Human nature makes us prone to suffering discomfort until it becomes unmanageable, rather than changing the stories to which we have become accustomed." Wanting to be right is one thing. Changing beliefs, which includes changing the neural pathways that support them, is quite another. Everybody wants to go to heaven. Nobody wants to die.

Blending with, and intentionally feeling into the source of discomfort, aligns the relationship of the personal with the universal. A story describing an alliance with the energy of change cultivates an entirely different world from a story that reacts defensively, resisting the energy of change. "Feeling the discomfort better," listening to and harmonizing with the information of disturbance and treating it as a message, makes us realize that we can experience energy as a benevolent source of power and guidance. It is a great love.

When attention is listening, discomfort functions as a wakeup call. Resistance to the energy of change metaphorically produces a different compound than adding harmony to the energy experiment. The alchemist's quest, transforming lead into gold, metaphorically parallels the pursuit of every religion and spiritual path—to achieve union with the divine. Listening in positive spirit, an Aiki alchemist purifies the lead of disturbance into the gold of usable informative energy. Union with the divine describes the alchemical transformation of the harbinger of discomfort into the creative power it heralds.

After the purification of identities, characters, and personas, as well as thought systems, beliefs, and attitudes, what remains directly radiates the experience of the central core, the original self, the essence of being, the divine spark. In the superposition of Aiki-land, the divine spark is both individual and universal at the same time. In a field encompassing this duality, energy shows its true intention and teleological essence, that of infinite, spontaneous creativity.

Conscious, intelligent choice grows out of conscious, intelligent perception of story and its influence. New information disturbs the existing order of synaptic patterning and asks the established story to have the courage to question itself. That courage comes by returning the focus of attention to experiencing the energy of the central core. In the founder's words, "Calm the spirit; return to source." As with breathing, once in the morning is not enough, because the story keeps changing.

With the acceleration of science, earlier imagined stories of Earth's position in the universe were replaced with new imagined stories. Around the time of the Renaissance, the very small group who paid attention to these things shifted the prevalent story to make the sun the universal center—an idea that had first been postulated centuries before Christ. Most people around the globe, however, continued to live in accordance with the older myths. Among those attuned to science, the heliocentric view persisted in popularity until around the time of the Enlightenment, when the next quantum leap occurred.

CREATIVITY'S DANCE PARTNER

A child is full of wonder. Both spiritual and scientific quest seek the fulfillment of that wonder. Stories of both religious experience and science have, for many, guided their entry into wonder and mystery. As stories get repeated, synaptic pathways deepen, holding power until something changes. Thought, by definition, lives in the past tense, thinking that it knows all, until something comes along implying that it doesn't.

As pathways deepen, becoming more established, knowledge crystallizes and becomes brittle in a way that begins to be threatened by inquiry. Then, as the quest for true science, divine knowledge, and the desire to live in God's heaven become institutionalized, almost inevitably, open uncertainty and spiritual inquiry degrade in favor of individuals maintaining power in the name of an institution.

When stories that reinforce mistaken understanding take over, thought ends up confusing myths and beliefs with reality. The church, rather than question its geocentric story of perfect circles, suppressed the ideas of a heliocentric universe and elliptical orbits, repressing and punishing individuals who espoused such thoughts. Attitudes of this kind were not limited to religious beliefs; there was similar resistance to new advancement among the guilds of science. This institutional behavior exemplifies a collective manifestation of a common human propensity when things thought to be known don't fit together with new information. This resistance is understandable when we look at the cost of rebuilding after the destruction of systems of thought.

In individuals, as in their institutions, as connection with wonder diminishes in favor of the illusory security of established knowledge or an established identity, a similar shift in focus occurs. The pure, unmitigated wonder of an infant crystallizes into a way of acting in the world, being seen, and interacting. This is the process through which an identity is created.

The process starts from creativity, and through repetition it develops a story that comes to be imagined by an individual as their identity. Yet this identity is a mirage, vapors of the self formed out of story by thinking identical thoughts over and over, triggering and calcifying an identical affect and identical postures and expressions. When we mistakenly confuse the identity for the self, identity becomes, in effect, an institution. Inquiry ebbs, and defensiveness grows.

In the face of incoherent or contradictory information, identity's first reaction defaults to defending the known. Within that amnesia, we forget that repeated verbal descriptions are both symbolic and hypnotic; habit, custom, and belief take command of the destiny of humanity. Without the inspiration of wonder, energy flows as it always has, formed out of the past. Stories become prisons of thought, capturing attention instead of serving creativity. Inquiry dies, leaving creativity with no dance partner.

The pervasiveness of an established pattern's influence, and the pathways that stories create from the moment of inception, exert inordinate influence. Absent sufficient creative life force, to live in established beliefs and habituated feelings seems the easiest thing in the world. Absent sufficient attention, one fails to notice or evaluate the cost of having to live there. Conscious awareness of the power and process of story changes the equation.

Creativity is harmonious relationship with Ki. The power of creativity naturally expresses itself, emanating from experiential connection to Ki. Vitality is free energy is creativity. The bio-electromagnetic energy of creation crystallizes in the manifest realm, appearing as a human being. Creativity takes on the colors, energetic tonality, or chemical makeup of the individual expressing it.

Consciously living in an interactive, dynamic universe where everything is relative, including perception, increases response ability.

Actively feeling the somatic aliveness of being guides attention into an ongoing, increasingly harmonious participatory relationship with the changing energy of a changing universe.

FEELING TRANSFORMS
FIGHT, FLIGHT, FREEZE INTO FLOW

In the story of relativity, change is the only constant. Newton's third law of motion, "action engenders equal and opposite reaction," pertains to any change in energy, story, feeling, or aesthetic, not just physical motion. Fixed beliefs, habituated feelings, and muscular patterns resist change. Negotiating change requires creativity, which comes out of resolving inner discord. The act of unifying attention and experience allows energy to be channeled through intent, coherent and unimpeded.

Unknown situations or challenges where established pathways no longer apply or function create the need for new synaptic connections, neural impulses, and muscular responses. Though the old stories may provide reference, the system's need for energy to establish new connections results in increased energy demand. A rush of Ki, activating at whatever level, shows up in the neural system as increased reactivity. Reactivity denotes an influx of Ki, in the same way the movement of leaves shows the otherwise invisible wind.

The resulting movement of subtler energies manifests as neural activity. Electric processes that release chemicals activating synaptic connections occur with simplicity and complexity along with a mysterious component. Medical science recognizes the phenomenon of the fight-flight-freeze syndrome, explaining it as the rush of adrenaline. Aiki study attunes a more original dimension of energy that acts "a second before," preceding and stimulating the rush of adrenaline.

In the martial metaphor, the increased rush of an unexpected attack can throw the system into overwhelm, impeding effective function. This in turn triggers a vicious cycle via an even greater adrenaline release, fight-or-flight response, and all the ensuing physiological activity. When resisted, the rush of energy can disturb whatever degree of connection exists between mind and body, causing the limited identity to default to input from the reptilian brain, without higher guidance. The reptilian brain's spectrum of options—freeze, avoid, or surge—limits the alive system's ability to create effective function.

The spectrum of computational power, from its origin to humanity's present level of consciousness, represents billions of years of evolution and expanding development. Recent evolutionary processes developed the prefrontal cortex, which mediates the reactive impulse, increasing the potential of intelligent response. We can engage in a process of unification by taking an intentional pause, counting to ten, and allowing time for the different aspects of the brain to unify into wholeness. This process produces function at a level that transcends the imagined capability of a fragmented brain or thought process.

In response to sudden, increased demand, the rush potentially empowers a breakthrough beyond previous limits and into greater connection with creativity and power. Or the pressure from resistance to the rush can instead cause increasing disassociation, driving attention to places quite opposite from the energy's original intent.

The resultant experience ranges on a continuum, where on one end we find "curiosity to interest," and on the other "discomfort to fear." Should the energy rush sufficiently overload the neural circuits, the system shuts down as a self-protective response. It is as if a circuit breaker were thrown, creating a deer-in-the-headlights scenario. Or, the surge may cause an explosive emotional loss of control. As the rush increases, at some level people will go temporarily mad, and in extreme cases they will totally, irreparably "lose their minds."

Aikido explores how to sail, surf, fly, or dance in this magical, overwhelming, incomprehensible universe of energy. Ki, pulsing through the system as bio-electromagnetic aliveness, flows through the center of being as the connection with the center of the universe. The resulting energy, when allowed and enjoyed, activates at an extraordinary level, thus coordinating new information, predicting future potential, and creating possible strategy for survival in a changing world.

Learning to surf the waves of life energy means continually adjusting position in relationship to the wave. The extraordinary skill and facility produced by precision presence increase our enjoyment in a positive, reciprocating cycle. Standing on the floating bridge of heaven enters each pulse of change creatively in positive spirit, enabling an increasingly innovative level of creativity.

Reactivity is an internal experience. The stimulus may be information about something that has already happened. Or it may be a challenge that needs to be addressed. Regardless, even and especially if action must be taken in the external world, job one is aligning ourselves in harmonious relationship with the internal energy source of the reactivity.

In every alive system, the pressure of the energy rush is ongoing. The constant disturbances can cause a loss of one's centered state. When the energy rush hits, brain activity and heartbeat speed up. As pressure builds, upsetting the system, connection to center and ground diminishes. The faster a potter's wheel goes, the more centered the clay that sits upon it needs to be. Any increase in energy requires an equal increase of precise attention to center and ground, to avoid ending up with "off the wall" behavior.

Sufficient electromagnetic energy emanating from a grounded central core radiates a sense of confidence and openness. When attention properly aligns with vitality, unseen channels open. Reciprocating echoes of possibility create innovative expression. An abundant quality of free energy improvises creative solutions at lightning speed in the face of the unknown, under life-and-death pressure.

Because Aiki focuses on blending with energy at the inception of its creation, a small shift of attention can cause a dramatic shift in outcome. Though influencing the universe may seem an overwhelming task, influencing life experience is not. The field of possibility changes relative to whether energy is channeled into identity's struggle for control or instead flows according to spirit's guidance, harmoniously absorbing and enjoying the unfolding wholeness.

FROM HELIOCENTRIC TO INTERGALACTIC COSMOLOGY

In the search that takes us back and forth between wonder and knowledge, science and technology continue to advance new understanding from which to create a new story. Around the time of the Enlightenment, enhanced telescopes and mathematics offered new information that pointed beyond the heliocentric picture of the universe to a larger reality, and the story evolved again to point to the center of the galaxy as the center of the universe.

The evolution didn't stop there, and it hasn't stopped yet. Presently, super-advanced telescopes sending pictures from outer space tell stories of incalculable galaxies and phenomena previously beyond imagination. An infinity of space seemingly without boundaries makes the concept of a center indefinable, and relativity the only frame of reference for motion. From geocentric to heliocentric to galactic to cosmic relativity, each understanding in turn generates an evolving interactive process of story and its effects. In our past, the stories were of monsters and gods, demons and magic forces and a flat, stable Earth. In the present story, not only is Earth not stable, the universe isn't either.

Science now tells the story of the Big Bang. According to this story—which is already being challenged, amended, and replaced—the universe, once a small, dense point of matter, "exploded" a little over a dozen billion years ago into an ever-expanding cosmos with a seemingly infinite number of galaxies. Setting aside the question of how a small, dense point of matter got "there," and where "there" is, astronomical stories are told by looking back into light from a distant past. The universal expansion, should that story prove correct, may have already reversed; if so, we have no way to know, because the information hasn't yet reached Earth.

An expanding universe implies a story in which some *thing* lies beyond the known universe of all existing matter and space, implying a re-definition the word *universe*. Of course, the word *thing* also misleads, without knowing into what dimension of creation the universe expands—if that is indeed what it does. For as we have seen, every story offers in effect only a limited description of a localized view of phenomena at a moment in time, from a relative position in relationship to perception.

The key is that a usable story isn't necessarily an accurate picture. Our present knowledge base exists light-years beyond earlier stories of a stable, stationary planet around which the universe revolved. For anyone with a modern education, the Earth spins in orbit around the sun, which swirls within a galaxy that is also moving through space at speeds incomprehensible to those who live on the surface of our planet. Still, for all practical purposes, life on Earth pretty much goes on in the long-held, imagined reality that the sun rises and sets, that things are stable and matter is solid.

The abstraction continues because of relativity. As one's motion and function are relatively the same as everything proximate, the idea of a stable planet applies as a relatively usable story. That's an important distinction. Stories captivate attention because they function to design an appropriate strategy for future action. The system as a unified field, properly balancing the story's accuracy in relation to its usefulness, increases capability and perception, thus enhancing prediction, strategy, and the effectiveness of action.

The formation of the cerebral structure develops from an evolutionary drive because knowing what to do can be a life-and-death issue. Accuracy or precision of description in the moment are secondary to serving story's primary purpose. Appearing to describe and explain what happened in the past, stories emerge as a basis for predicting correct action in an unknown future.

Science and religion have acted as both complementary and antagonistic processes attempting to solve humanity's challenge of divining a correct path, whether for a specific action or for one's life. Religious belief has been, for many, a primary source for answering the question of what to do. Numerous and varied thought systems around the globe each create a code of morals, thereby inducing behaviors that please the divine or scientifically align with nature.

Some beliefs and religions imagine a system of law, punishment, and reward that is administered by the divine, commonly an anthropomorphized creator of the universe who works in mysterious ways. Science, peering through another lens of reference and understanding, tells an entirely different story and speaks from yet another universe of imagination. Currently, the science of quantum mechanics tells stories of a theory of a unified field, an unfolding creative union of forces manifesting the universe, which work in mysterious ways.

Fixed opinions lack creativity and too often argue and fight for dominance. Scientific and religious beliefs express the nature of creativity in that they are as diverse as scientists and religious believers. Naturally, they see different things. They are looking at reality from different positions. When differing viewpoints engage in dialogue, the universe manifests creativity. Harmonious relationship, always present in the field of potential, brings creative power into the manifest realm. When one person thinks something different, this generates ripple effects, which unfold into a changing story, creating a different experience of the universe and quality and color of life.

CROSSING THE CHASM

Around the turn of the twentieth century, the story of relativity dramatically changed the foundation of imagination yet again. As countless galaxies seem to open to an endless infinity beyond imagination, the subatomic world explores its own incomprehensible mystery. With the equation $E=mc2$ and the advent of quantum mechanics, the previous understanding of physics dissolves into an unimaginable realm, confounding the laws of the classical world.

Though relativity and quantum theory don't agree, they cross and encompass the chasm between the physics of particles and the physics of fields, between matter and energy. In looking to resolve the discrepancies in relativity and quantum mechanics, attempts to explain the process of creation science presently explore a story calling the theoretical creator of the universe a "unified field."

According to a mythic theory from modern physics, the universe comes into existence through the mysterious amalgamation of four identified forces participating as an interpenetrating unified field. In this story, all four forces must be present, and creation does not come into being without any one of the forces. Science can distinguish between them but presently cannot explain the mysterious interrelationship.

The four forces—the electromagnetic force, gravity, and the weak and strong forces—combine, both creating and being created by the universal field. The strong force holds the nucleus of the atom together. Close to the center, it is a powerful force, but its power diminishes rapidly over any distance. The weak force, which operates over short ranges, is subtle in influence. The electromagnetic force governs the attraction between electrons and the nucleus, stabilizing atomic structures. Gravity is centripetal, moving or tending to move toward a center, and generates the power of attraction within the sphere of influence of a given mass or field. The mystery remains in finding a unifying context for the four forces that have been identified in the unified field theory.

Of course, the word *force* misleads when we don't know what preceded, created, or sustains the initial vibration on which creation is built. Nobel Prize–winning quantum physicist Richard Feynman has been quoted as saying, "I think I can safely say that nobody understands quantum mechanics."

Quantum theory, while its accuracy is still questionable, is a usable story leading to phenomenal scientific and technological advancement. A story's ultimate value in the human sphere draws from its function, not its clarity or verity.

In the art of Aikido, the unified field theory becomes the unified field experience—not theoretical, experiential. The strong force, referred to in this study as *center*, represents the vital energy of the central core of aliveness. It defines the central power of being, mysterious in its source, mysterious in its mission. It implies dynamic presence and coherence, a being with weight, substance, and influence.

The weak force, renamed the subtle force, refers to harmonious interaction of the central core with every relationship energetic and material, hidden and manifest, and is referred to in the study as *circle*. The electromagnetic force represents the radiance of vitality. Every cell of the body, like every subatomic particle, exudes charm. The electromagnetic force is the extension of Ki, intention into action.

Gravity equates in the experiential realm with the cultivation of the spirit of attraction spoken of by the founder of Aikido. Energy follows attention, magnetizing into life the objects and qualities of thoughts and attention, the aspects that come under the sway of the subtle force. The spirit of attraction draws the forces, causing a remixing of the chemicals or reblending of the colors, feelings, or qualities that make up a person and a life experience.

When the four unify symphonically, the exalted workings, Mita Hiraki in Japanese, come together and in concert open a path before the mind's eye, offering guidance on the journey of life. The literal meaning is: *mita*, "seen" (with the eyes); *hiraki*, "opening" (as one opens a door in the mind's eye, or as a path opens before one). The whisperings of the exalted workings guide the way to harmonious relationship with the forces that create life and the universal energies that sustain it.

When faced with a challenge, the electromagnetic force of the alive system sends out a question that echoes into the universe. The answer shows up as energy that floods the system. The intention and intelligence of universal energy echo through the whole of creation, in what Osensei called "the echo of the universal Ki." The guidance and wisdom of the divine each flow as energy that echoes between every being and the creative force of the universe.

3

THE UNIFIED FIELD

Gull cuts through the fog

as if it weren't really there . . .

Just so, our fears.

Chris Thorsen

THE WORLD ACCORDING TO PHYSICS

On the leading edge of science and technology, understanding and application, and redefining reality, physics explores the laws of nature, the forces shaping the world. The impact of science and technology has been the dominant force of change in our human existence. The difference between human existence at a primitive level and the present heights of technological society spans millennia of change, though most of this has occurred in the last centuries. The quest for knowledge accelerating dramatically at ever-increasing speeds has virtually changed everything; yet at the same time, as always, the fundamentals remain in place.

Science and technology represent and describe the complementary domains of pure science and applied science. The purpose of pure science is pure wonder, inquiry, and exploration. Pure science investigates the universe, creating knowledge and understanding about what the universe is, how it came into being, and how it functions. Applied science uses knowledge to functionally change the techniques and technologies with which we live our lives, in this way theoretically improving our experience. Pure science, exploration, and curiosity about the mystery of creation serve a practical function in their relevance to applied science, which in turn pushes the limits of pure science.

A wholesome reciprocity ensues in the two forms of science going back and forth, each developing the other, and thus the magic of creation unfolds, $1 + 1 = 1$. In iterations of synergistic interplay, wonder and knowledge enhance each other, changing what science means, expanding both the topics and methods of study. As the boundary between energy and matter dissolves, so too do the borders between disciplines of study. As science drifts into the areas of consciousness, awareness, and attention, *what* and *how* approach, ever so tentatively, the philosophical domain of *why*.

Vibration, pulsation, and the back-and-forth between polarities lead to completion both of the universe and of the actions of everyday life. The back-and-forth between knowledge and wonder, meaning and experience, causes story to change.

The atom, once perceived as the smallest particle of solid matter, indivisible and existing in a specific position, is currently understood as a mysterious arcana, a complex interplay of phenomena. The entities identified as subatomic particles, when explored in the quantum world, behave more like spooky fields of potential. Though "no one understands" quantum mechanics, and though it seemingly contradicts the laws of classical physics, application of quantum mechanics has transformed technological innovation, imagination, and the stories functioning as the software that makes meaning out of life experience.

At the subatomic level, there are moments when an electron reaches a bifurcation point. When the energy builds up sufficiently, an electron will jump to the next electron ring, shell, or orbit. At the human level, as the bio-electromagnetic force of Ki flow increases, it potentially enables the jump to the next experiential level of consciousness, mental clarity, power, and precision action. When the light of attention shines into the unknown, vitality builds until there is enough Ki available to actualize a quantum leap to the next realm of potential, whether in the realm of action or understanding.

The buildup of energy as well as the jump itself can be quite disturbing. In fact, that is its intent—but for a good reason. A sense of disturbance precedes every shift in the development of consciousness because everything is activated by Ki. Everything runs on energy. The whole system not only runs on energy but, as it turns out, *is* energy, which invites a reevaluation not only of the terms we use but also of the thinking that created them.

Human consciousness, as a collective experience of transformational moments, each usually presaged by great art or great wars, or both at the same time. Though change is always happening in the story of thought and understanding, the accelerating pace keeps increasing, raising its impact in the sphere of human meaning.

THE VOYAGE HOME

Science, questioning whether the way something looks is the way it really is, reimagines thinking—though not for everyone. Only a very small percentage of the populace had to actually study science in order for the changing stories of so few to so affect the lives of so many. Most people have little interest in reconciling the dynamic between the theories of relativity and quantum mechanics. Few even know it exists. Humanity as a collective spends little time thinking about the infinity of space and the subatomic world, whether the universe is expanding, or the question of What Is Going On if solid matter doesn't really exist, because these areas of inquiry have little direct effect on day-to-day life.

Yet life on this planet is constantly being changed by ripples in thought and evolutions in story, even if these changes are imperceptible to most. Generally, the motion is gradual enough that it goes unattended, until the potential increase in the wave trough's back-and-forth vibration reaches a sufficient level of dynamic tension, creating the next quantum leap. In the back-and-forth between parts of some presently unknowable essence, energy builds, disturbing the field; and at some point, as an electron "jumps" to the next orbit, things potentially change. In everyday life, none of that directly matters much . . . until it does.

Until the change in story produces a change in the application of science affecting daily life, the world seems to know or care little, and understandably so. Even those who value the accuracy and insight each new story offers will fundamentally continue to live in a functional story, based on how the world looks from their relative position. Effective function prevails over accurate description.

The reason that it doesn't matter much to most people is that an infinitesimally small percentage of people had to face the challenges and hardships of the spice trail for virtually the whole world to eventually add spice to their life. Once the adventurers blazed the trail, to change world cuisine everyone else simply had to walk to the market.

It is not necessary to train in Aikido techniques on the mat, or to understand relativity or quantum mechanics, in order to enhance the flavor of life's changing stories with spicy informational possibilities such as new art and new discoveries. One does not need to comprehend space to move through space so as to position oneself in a more functional location. Nor is it necessary to study or understand psychology to re-cognize and move to a preferable location emotionally, to discern what feels better.

One does not need to understand how an apple manifests to assimilate its nourishment. To do so, however, one must eat the apple. In a similar way, the central core and the circle need not be understood for us to experience feeling that we are part of the unified field of the unfolding mystery. Yet to do so, one must stand on the floating bridge that activates potential. A first breath of feeling a part of a larger creation begins the process of relinking. Sensing into the field where more exists than appears on the screen of awareness, opens connection to the power of listening.

It is easy to forget, yet important to remember, that nothing is separate; everything is a part of the life-energy process. The evolutionary and genetic development that produces every individual goes back in time and projects forward in time as an unbroken whole. Sense of interconnectedness with the totality, the visceral sensation of being both a product of history and the potential future of the life process, gets lost in the ambient light of life's daily pressures.

The unified field of being, the mysterious field that creates and sustains the cosmos, is birthed out of focusing attention viscerally, experiencing being part of the absolute, the mysterious field that creates and sustains the cosmos. Feeling, sinking, and opening into something beyond the known all transform experience. To feel into the infinite that exists beyond understanding can be understood as prayer.

Prayer, in its best form, is conversation with the creative force of the universe, a communication relinking an individual with the source of creation. Prayer is incomplete when it only involves asking; it becomes complete by listening to the answer, in the breath and feelings, in thought and spirit. Prayer issues forth through the quantum looking glass and completes through whole-being listening in harmonious spirit, or in other words, giving one's whole attention to the essential guidance of the exalted workings.

In the manifest world, as the mundane issues of everyday life absorb consciousness, it is easy to forget to feel part of a vast universe; it is easy to shy from the unknown vastness. From the perspective of someone with a limited system of thought or belief, a known or fixed identity, entering the vastness can seem overwhelming or even terrifying. Yet from the point of view of the vastness itself, it is neither of these things; it is simply vastness.

Living into the manifest realm, while at the same time experientially reconnecting to the totality, causes us to remember the fragments as the whole. Feeling a part of the whole puts life in perspective, leading us to develop positive neural pathways and enlightening stories. And when we do so consistently, repeatedly, and religiously, this forms the basis or origin of religious practice.

When a high-speed, life-threatening attack occurs, everything is stripped away but the essence of the moment. Only the outcome matters: reaching the top of the mountain. The path taken does not matter, nor does the name one gives to the mountain. Once the individual enters experiential quantum entanglement with the universal, the song one sang on the journey there is not that important.

Connection to the totality is part of the life-energy process and is not something grasped in the mind. It doesn't happen via thought. The act of experientially engaging in the whole of creation begins as a feeling. When this feeling occurs, it is an experiential sense of being, a visceral feeling interpenetrating with the whole. It comes to us through the field that unifies mind and body in the realm of the spirit. We may start to sense it in the imagination, but it only activates when experience includes and unifies with the physical realm, simultaneously felt through the somatic sense of being.

Feeling is flavored toward fear or wonder through the spices that are available to intent, and cooked to perfection in the fire of practice. There are a few spices that should be in everyone's kitchen. The vital spices from quantum mechanics include: wave particle duality, uncertainty, superposition, quantum entanglement, and the unified field theory. Resonant principles from Aikido include: Ki flow, harmony, presence, centering, grounding, entering, and blending. All these "spices" can be applied to enrich the flavor of life, transforming wave particle duality into wave particle unity.

Aikido and quantum mechanics have opened new playgrounds of exploration that they now offer to human consciousness. Once adventurers blaze the trail, everyone else can simply walk to the market creating a beautiful world of harmony, by focusing the center of attention into the center of experience, and focusing the aliveness of consciousness into the vitality of the alive system, the feeling or glow of life itself.

WAVE PARTICLE DUALITY:
IT IS AND IT ISN'T—BOTH AND NEITHER

To simplify the story, light appears as either a wave or a particle, energy or matter, depending on how it is observed and how the experiment is set up. In other words, light appears to be both, potentially implying that both states exist, unobserved, as aspects of an inclusive wave particle unity: a dimension encompassing the sum of its parts. The quantum shift changed science, bringing consciousness into the paradigm. Science, in trying to understand the structure of light, found several answers instead of just one, thus opening up a whole library of new questions.

Quantum mechanics describes a field of energy potential collapsing and a particle coming into existence through observation, prior to which it seemingly exists as . . . nobody knows, so there is no word for it. So in the meantime, exploiting the most convenient term, scientists refer to it as a *field* of potential. Yet the wave, particle, or the whatever it is when it's both or neither, exists at the same time in both forms, or goes back and forth so fast between the two that it appears to exist simultaneously as both. It is both or neither, or, in a mysterious way, something else altogether. Quantum Aikido might view it as the wave particle unity, which emphasizes the importance of training oneself to have a harmonious relationship with the mystery.

A realm where matter and energy are simultaneously two separate things and also the same thing, originally of the same source, exists in dimensions beyond the comprehension of the existing paradigms of classical scientific thought. When we understand that duality exists in the mind of the observer, we fuel movement beyond fixed beliefs into creative thinking. In the quantum world, polarities exist as a unified field. Standing on the floating bridge of heaven enriches the evolving relationship between the known world and the mystery. When practiced as a way of travel, the proper path and destination are achieved in the completion of either a simple task or the whole of life's journey.

Life depends on how one sets up the experiment. The experimenter defines what data the experiment will measure. The process of activating experience happens through the quality, location, or focus of attention. Where someone is coming from affects what will be looked at and colors how it will be looked at. As the wave potential collapses into a particle, seemingly as a result of observation, the energy potential of life crystallizes relative to how each situation is looked at.

Once an experiment is set up a given way, possibility collapses within those parameters. The infinite potential of an individual collapses into story. The patterns that become identity, persona, and character form through hierarchical organization of selected information and the habitual, near-identical repetition of the patterning. Operating from the mindset that life is a struggle, infinite potential collapses into magnetics and dynamic tension, reinforcing those overtones. In the return to source, other possibilities exist.

The consciousness of the observer and how the experiment is set up are fundamental pivot points of Wave Particle Duality, which reinforce and expand the understanding that what our thoughts experience as truth about reality is in fact merely one of a variety of potential descriptions. Any subjective observation of experience is colored by point of view, mood, and focus of attention. In a world of uncertainty where matter and energy cannot be differentiated or explained, only described, an objective observer does not exist.

UNCERTAINTY

Heisenberg's uncertainty principle grew out of the impossibility of tracking both the speed and location of an electron at the same time. In the subatomic world, science is unable to predict where an electron exists. The uncertainty principle had been postulated centuries earlier in the lexicon of the church as "God works in mysterious ways." Uncertainty, another portal into the field of imagination, acknowledges that objective observation is an imaginary construct, a story.

In classical science, speed, position, and predictability are virtual facts. In the quantum world, science can only predict where an electron *might* exist. Newton identified laws, as if things exist in a specific position in a solid universe. Even Einstein's world of relativity generally followed common sense laws, though it did start to bend space-time. Niels Bohr, one of the thought leaders in quantum physics, lived in another zone altogether and explored a world that was beyond strange.

Without knowing whether a phenomenon is a particle or not, covering the quandary with the word *energy* doesn't change the fact that there is no certainty to exactly what it is, let alone where it is. Uncertainty, along with the other insights and principles surfacing out of quantum mechanics, presently reinforces and amplifies the appearance of, and encourages the acceptance of, the source of creation as a mystery. A mystery is something about which one is uncertain. The classical mind attempted to *explain* the mystery. To enter the quantum world means to explore *expanding* the mystery, loving living into the ambiguity.

To understand the workings that created the universe may be beyond the grasp of the human mind at its current stage of development. Until and unless evolution or development changes that, it leaves human knowledge a long way from comprehending how either the universe or the workings that created the universe got here, with all their implications and echoing ramifications. The bigger the body of knowledge, the bigger the questions.

With a shortage of the availability of free energy, people live in their stories as if they were certain, avoiding, resisting, or denying the unknown. A field of potential also exists where knowledge and uncertainty create an alliance. The question is, who gets to write the story, and how will they write it? That question goes back to the alignment of attention's relationship with experience, creating the state of being and quality of person that will create the technology of story and the story of technology.

The mystery is the source of all beauty as well as creation itself. It implies the ability to accept that truth, reality, WIGO, and the one source don't always have to make sense according to any familiar story. That story is just a story.

Attention to a relationship of quantum harmony, rather than solving the mystery, unifying with it and getting to know the mystery better, is the doorway to elegance in producing a fulfilling life. It is a common misunderstanding that in the face of the incomprehensible, the brain functions to create certainty. In fact the reverse is true. This misunderstanding may be the result of a programming error, because the brain's job is solving problems, figuring out what to do. It was never intended to solve the great mystery. Living into the unknown is the privilege of those unable to resist that mysterious calling.

SUPERPOSITION

In quantum mechanics, superposition describes the possibility of an electron potentially existing in two or more energy states of different velocities, or in multiple locations at the same time. Another one of the incomprehensible facets of quantum physics, superposition seems impossible according to the view of classical physics as it applies to the surface of the planet. Like wave particle duality and the science of quantum mechanics in general, superposition implies another domain of energy or a dimension of existence manifesting invisibly in both realms in the same time-space, seemingly existing beyond imagination or conception.

Superposition in thought suggests the ability to hold multiple contrasting thoughts or feelings simultaneously. In the realm of the spirit, superposition changes the location of attention from defensively holding a fixed worldview to embracing a perspective full of wonder and exploring an infinite, interactive creation of potential in constant flux. A state of being that, in the world of duality, looks like being in two places at once is in the quantum dimension: the unified field experience, standing on the floating bridge of heaven.

Being in two places at the same time allows us to locate the center of attention somatically, viscerally, and experientially, deep in the very center of the glow of aliveness, while at the same time participating in external reality, or the circle. The power of vitality, channeled through the focus of attention, expresses itself as masterful action in harmonious relationship to change. Activating attention and experience as a unified field, inter-unifying the two into one, converts energy into capability. Standing on the floating bridge of heaven unifies knowledge and power, transforming dynamic potential into creativity.

Polarities that are fundamentally opposed to each other can produce extraordinary vision when allowed to express themselves creatively in harmony, in dialogue, in conception, and in function—just as quantum insights have done in the world of classical science. Disintegrating the limitations of understanding births the possibility of enjoying experiential interplay with the collective charm of reality. We move from position to superposition, transitioning into the quantum world and the energy universe, where the self mysteriously unifies the divine and manifest realms and comes to exist in both locations at the same time.

Aikido's superposition explores the process of experiencing harmonious relationship between the known and the unknown, the individual and the totality, the personal and the universal, one's inner experience and the external aspects of existence. In Aikido, superposition experiences attention located in thinking and feeling, aligning the inner while functioning in the external world at the same time.

QUANTUM ENTANGLEMENT

Quantum entanglement posits that subatomic particles can be mysteriously connected, transcending space-time. Despite distances across space of billions of light-years, a change induced in one will occur in the other "at the same time." Einstein reacted against the idea of two things being one thing at the same time, famously terming quantum entanglement "spooky action at a distance."

The quantum world bridges the threshold between and beyond form and flow, and exists in an uncertain, ever-changing, interrelated, and counterintuitive universe. Here, potential fields and spooky possibility allow inexplicable interconnections. Indra's net, an ancient myth from Hindu lore, metaphorically symbolizes an infinite, omnipresent web of entanglements and interdependencies that interconnect all aspects of creation. The interrelationship allows each jewel appearing at each node of the net to reflect a microcosm of the whole.

Experience and meaning are in quantum entanglement, each affecting the other at the same time and through time-space. Reactivity triggers quantum entanglement every time a stimulus occurs. Aiki quantum entanglement simultaneously designs and executes the appropriate action at the optimal time. If there's any truth to the concept of a unified field, or to the mystical teachings of earlier religions, the whole of creation expresses quantum entanglement at once, between all matter and forces in existence.

The idea that particles or fields are interconnected beyond the limitations of space-time, when combined with the ideas of wave particle duality, uncertainty, and superposition, adds to the circumstantial case for the unified field theory of interconnectedness, oneness, or a single source of creation. Story gives names to such theories, and people fight over whose story is true. But a mysterious, cosmic phenomenon by any other name . . . brings the universe into existence.

UNIFIED FIELD THEORY

Science has moved from the illusion of a stable Earth and solid matter to exploring the quantum story, where subatomic particles vaporize into, and appear out of, fields of energy potential. The unified field theory introduced in the mid-twentieth century was an attempt to reconcile the discrepancies between classical science, relativity, and quantum mechanics. The story of a unified field of four forces—strong, weak, electromagnetic, and gravitational—remains an uncertain theory, yet to be proven; but currently this story holds a central position, even as variations and alternatives continue to spawn and may eventually supplant it.

In the unified field experience, the unification of the four forces creates the experience of being. To restate briefly, the four forces are the strong force that assembles the central core of being; the subtle force that conducts every relationship, circling the aliveness of the center; gravity, the force of attraction that draws energies into orbit and experience into life; and electromagnetic radiation, which expresses the reciprocating echoes of charm that are broadcast out into creation.

In the realm of physics, everything is said to affect everything. That is equally true in the realm of the spirit. Quantum entanglement, spooky action at a distance, implies that quantum super-entanglement, the floating bridge of heaven, is WIGO. The interconnected quantum entanglement of the totality exists experientially, with or without the mathematics to explain it to the mind of science.

Energies interpenetrate in a unified field of being, thus creating the hologram of human experience. Analogous to the creator in other myths, the unified field experience mysteriously manifests the exalted workings, the universal whisperings. Understanding may offer value in helping one choose what to do with one's life. The knowledge alone has value only as a starting point.

Experiential presence and extraordinary listening translate the whisperings of guidance that cross the chasm and turn knowledge into action, actualized in effective application. Life is enjoyed and its nourishment assimilated by attention to breathing, inspiration, and assimilating the vitality, as well as eating the energy through feeling, and viscerally processing aliveness into experience.

Even through tremendous change the fundamentals remain the

same, leaving consciousness where it formed originally. Consciousness, whatever story it may tell itself, has always lived on the threshold of the mystery. Breathing harmony with the universal pulse of the mystery activates creative innovation. The spiritual journey a warrior travels into the center of the central core transforms potential discomfort from the pressure of vital force, turning it instead into guidance, power, and contribution. Feeling emanates from the one source, a field of harmony, and gives birth to movement that expresses life as a joyful dance.

MUSUBI: TYING IT ALL TOGETHER

The Japanese term *musubi* translates loosely as "to tie together." Aikido studies how to "unify the field" experientially through musubi: connection, unification, and reconciliation. Aiki adds the concept of *Ki*, using the phrase *Ki-musubi*. Ki-musubi, in the practice of the waza, the set of techniques formally understood by the general public as Aikido, implies tying one's Ki to the Ki of an attacker.

In the Do, Ki-musubi implies joining attention with vitality, spirit with Ki, the individual with the universal, and the manifest world with the divine, thus unifying all creation with the mystery. Aiki explores the relationship tying the individual and society with the forces of energy that create life and sustain the universe.

Musubi suggests power that magically unites atoms. Theoretically in modern physics, an unknown power that in the interim we call "the unified field" gravitationally magnetizes together in mysterious ways, and appears to create the universe. Musubi describes the phenomenon tying together the unity, connection, or interpenetration of the four forces in modern physics that create the universe, according to that creation myth.

In music, musubi ties notes together in harmony, creating a unifying resonance. In Aikido, Ki and musubi unify the forces and workings, and infinite techniques of the art appear. And in the realm of the spirit, the exalted workings glow through the self. A single source—*Ichi Rei,* commonly translated as "one spirit" or less commonly as "one light"—illuminates the path through feelings, thoughts, magnetism, gravity, and yet-unrecognized forms of universal energy.

Awareness of the *location* of attention opens the option of positioning attention in a location of better feelings, turning knowledge into power. The founder spoke of "not something new, something more original." Each step tying attention deeper into central core enhances the power drawn from the origin of creation.

Aikido explores experiencing the vibrational back-and-forth between the relationship of individual consciousness and the echoes of universal Ki, leading into oneness. Feeling unifies the experience of both in the same time-space, thereby freeing energy. Energy potential, when released from bondage to past patterning, transforms enhancing capability. Awareness, refined into attention, continues positioning itself in the dynamic center of the center of the central core. When finer dimensions align, awareness develops and masters the ability to see "subtler colors" or dimensions, out of which emerge innovative, coherent action, appropriate to changing circumstances.

Transforming life from a struggle to a dance, a spirit of confluence changes conflict into creativity, fulfilling one's mission and dreams. To balance central core of being with its orbiting relationships inevitably guides intelligent strategy, leading to a coherent life experience. An emotionally positive tone brings forth an open mind, giving birth to infinite innovation. Creativity empowers living life in harmony with the calling of essential self, the journey of spirit to completion. Life unfolds symphonically. God is in heaven. All is right with the world.

RELATIVELY RELATIVE RELATIVITY

Aikido can be a practice applied in the martial realm, developing skill in how to handle a physically violent situation. It can also be a process of aligning in harmony with the world. A spirit of harmony opens a doorway, initially for an individual and potentially for all life on the planet.

Aikido provides an alternative to the continuum of fighting or giving up. Fighting in a zero-sum game, as if either winning or losing were the only options, generates a defensive posture instead of a creative one. Harmoniously, from a larger perspective, positive spirit postulates a third option, distilling, absorbing, and applying the inherent learning in a situation. The ability to influence the outcome of any situation is enhanced through working in harmony with what is. As a spirit of harmony enters every situation, challenge, encounter, and negotiation, it brings the ability to generate the seed crystal in a positive spirit of harmonizing with the changing movement of the universal.

Aikido realizes the potential development from reactivity into a dynamic field of love. Osensei taught that practice should "bear fruit in the world." Sections of the globe are living in wars that have existed for centuries, some for millennia. Unfortunately, synaptic patterning can commit so much energy to a fixed mindset that there is not enough Ki left to do anything different. When we tell a story of fragmentation, a story that reproduces pain from eras past, it ends up producing ever-greater pain in the future—until and unless the story changes. It could. It is just a story.

The potential of other stories exists in the unified field, stories of working together to create peace and harmony. Their invocation requires energy to activate. Without sufficient Ki, free energy, it is as if there were no other options, which as quantum mechanics teaches is both true and not true at the same time, depending on how one looks at it.

A story that identifies with only part of the system, generating fragmentation, puts the forces in the system into opposition with one another. Yet when we tie the fragments together experientially by standing on the floating bridge, we find that wisdom and compassion, universal spirit and individual creativity, appear as a felt sense, emerging through the vital energetic center of being.

The art of peace, as it enters the unknown and melds into the magic of creativity, begins by winning over the discord in one's own mind. From there it spreads, affecting consciousness as one candle lights another. The free energy of creativity activates the unified field and serves to redefine being, and with it the quality of human relationship and the foundations of society.

Within the mystery of the unified field, creation and its source, the known and the unfolding dissolve into re-cognizing each other, changing the story and the world. When we feel into the energy rush, pressure translates into a calling that relinks attention to the source of power and guidance. Warrior spirit explores feeling better as an operating process. Harmony, reconciliation, unification, and peace are the fundamental watchwords tying the practice together.

THE CULTIVATION OF THE SPIRIT OF ATTRACTION AND THE CURVATURE OF TIME-SPACE

Watching someone skilled in the art of Aikido, it seems too easy, fake. It doesn't make sense without understanding the concept of leading Ki, the energy that forms into intention, creating any action. Any intention creates an attraction to its goal. An attacker's intention creates an attraction to the target.

As stated previously, the Japanese term *musubi* means "to tie together." Once someone commits to an attack, they have tied their energy to the target of the attack. Aikido responds by returning the favor through Ki-musubi, harmoniously tying the Ki of the practitioner to the Ki of the attacker, leading both to peaceful reconciliation. In the physical practice, centrifugal power is created by moving "off the line" of an attack, causing the attacker to redirect their intent as they turn, changing their direction. The change in direction creates a circular motion that allows the dispersion of the force without anyone ending up a victim of it. Moving the point of focus, the target (one's physical structure in this case), leads to the magnetic attraction of the attacker's focused energy.

As an attacker turns, readjusting to the target's new position and creating a new direction, the centrifugal motion gravitationally changes reality, in effect causing a curvature of time-space. The flow of the combined forces leads the energy. In effect, the momentum of the movement performs the technique. Variations in the kaleidoscopic interactions between the forces generate seemingly infinite possibilities.

For scientists, the physics of quantum mechanics opened a completely new level of understanding and mystery beyond the paradigm of classical science. Likewise, the founder of Aikido opened a path before the world, teaching that Aikido's exalted workings lead individuals to fulfillment and function in service of the completion of the universe. His description of Aikido as the realization of love was a quantum leap in the world of martial arts, placing Aikido in the superposition of being both a martial as well as a Venusial art, an art in the realm of Venus the goddess of love.

LANGUAGE, THOUGHT, AND
THE POETRY OF PROSE

The process of learning requires entering the unknown. Otherwise, only additive knowledge is gained that doesn't disturb the existing order or change present descriptions.

Human consciousness has moved from the geocentric worldview, to the heliocentric, to the galactic, to the universal; from atoms, to subatomic particles, to fields of potential; and no one knows what story the next religious awakening or scientific epiphany will bring. Every new discovery expands the dawn of awakening consciousness, pushing it further into the unknown, beyond outdated modes of thought and understanding. With the advent of new breakthroughs in science and art, new language forms as a way of sharing stories that surface in human awareness.

As the exploration of the mystery expands, the dynamics of the process creating it exceed language. This is at least in part because they exceed knowledge. Approaching the unknown, where language does not yet exist, stories lean on myths and metaphors, analogies and similes. New words and meanings are created. Existing words are used and understood in new ways as knowledge and understanding increase.

People tend to think of the meanings of words as being fixed. Like astronomers looking into light from the past, the dictionary defines words based on how they have been used. Usage changes over time. It is not only the universe that is evolving. So is human understanding of it. And so is language evolving to "talk story" about it all.

In a world of law, conversations are had and contracts are written as if words were set or had fixed meanings. Words are not fixed in stone. They change with time and usage. They are colors on an artist's palette. Words represent. They can never truly encompass the concepts being explored. Words can point the way to new possibilities that each person must explore experientially. Like the concept of attention, a word will never encompass the meaning; it can only open the portal to creative worlds of expanding meaning.

The early stages of brain development establish the seed crystal of story for the higher cortical functions. Samuel Bois, in his book *The Art of Awareness*, describes the evolution of human consciousness through five stages: The first is magical thinking. Everything is explained as magic. The second stage is binary, where everything is either right or wrong. The third is a stage where consciousness begins to open to multiple possibilities. The fourth reveals the intertwinement and potential inner connection of those multiple visions. And the fifth is described as understanding the multiplicity as aspects of a totality. A large portion of the system of human thought and language is presently formed in an adversarial, stage-two, simplistic paradigm of right and wrong, good versus evil. The majority of the world still lives dominated by that stage of the development of awareness. Looking through that lens inevitably exacerbates conflict.

As consciousness develops, we potentially peer through a different lens, and confluence becomes possible. The opposites in a system needn't remain at odds with each other. Like polarities functioning as a unified field by universal law, they complete each other. The opposite poles and a magnetic field unfold together, creating and completing both each other and the field. Feeling, intentionally paying attention to experience, or heightening sensory acuity, activates a natural proprioceptive process unifying seemingly incongruous forces. Together these forces manifest the system, a totality, a universe, and creation itself.

In the quantum world of infinite potential, words have potential meaning depending on how they're sent. Their transmission is, in effect, a field of potential meaning, which collapses into imagined understanding depending on how it is observed or received. The meaning only appears solid or stable for a while. Eventually a commonality of understanding allows the words of the new language to establish themselves.

Until a new lexicon is created, new insights remain the Tao that cannot be spoken, at least in prose. As we stand on the floating bridge between the known and exploration, communication takes place in a field of potential meaning. In the exploration of the quantum world, poetic imagery offers a magic carpet for the journey through the infinite mystery of creation.

Neither thought nor language can ever encompass the infinite, multidimensional, unfolding complexity of creation. Its dimensionality, totality, and interdependent interaction is incomprehensible and as such beyond indescribable. A linear string of words can only refer attention toward, and approximate, reality. No matter. Call it poetry, imagery that evokes a response in feeling and experience. When a story passes beyond entering the unknown of the imagination and that which sources the imagination, and into the incomprehensible ambiguity of the unknowable, the transmission is poetry.

ECHOING EFFECTS

A different story gives birth to a different interactive experience, bringing forth a different reality. Effects rhyme with the poetry of the stories that create them. In the days when humanity operated from the illusion of central position, seeing a geocentric world with an imaginary stable center, variations of "the divine right of kings" were pervasive as forms of government.

As the idea of the universe and an interrelated system in motion became a common story, ideology changed. Shifting ideas of government emerged, challenging the idea of power exercised from a central position. New paradigms of reason, individualism, and skepticism flourished, and democratic monarchies appeared as part of the transition. During the Enlightenment, the pace and quality of knowledge and change accelerated dramatically. Democracies began to proliferate.

By the twentieth century, a multi-galactic universe was the commonly accepted science. The once-experimental concept of democracy became so dominant a form of government that even countries ruled by dictators often called themselves "democracies" or "people's republics"—even as these authoritarian regimes inhibited freedom of speech, information, and the press. In effect, these extreme measures taken by such regimes in their attempts to control public dialogue only further emphasize the power and significance of story.

Within an individual, a fixed or authoritarian mindset will similarly bind creativity, and individuals stuck in this mindset will also resort to extreme measures. When defensiveness unconsciously claims its authority by repetition and habituation, and thus limits listening and learning, the oxygen of creativity is cut off. In the absence of awareness regarding ingrained patterns, they rule unchallenged.

Fixation, tension, and resistance, once viscerally experienced, begin releasing. In proportion to the shift of attention into feeling, muscle tension relaxes, breathing deepens, and heart and brain waves slow. Physiologically, the systems of life entrain the harmony affecting the finer dimensions. When attention is freed from fixed patterns, Ki that had habitually channeled into established pathways dissolves into flow. Indeterminate microvolts of "free energy" return to the field of potential. Every rush of energy and every burst of reactivity reinforces an old habit or pattern, or opens new possibilities. Attention to developing habit patterns enhances the possibility of conscious influence.

Mysteriously, energy creating and permeating the universe flows through the central core of being. The glow of the central core, the strong force, radiates connection with the circle, the subtle force, which balances all the aspects and relationships of life that surround and engage with the central core. In an earlier teaching, humanity was offered a somewhat similar path to heaven, which one might paraphrase as: "Love thy circle as thy central core"—not more than, not less than. The important aspect is the balance between the two forces until $1 + 1 = 1$; they dance as a unified field.

On the threshold of the polarity of domains, where the known borders the mystery, pressure builds from time to time, as might occur between any couple with differences. The potential dynamic is ever present. When out of balance, opposition becomes a potential field for argument, absorbing creativity and telling stories from a conflicted operating place. War, whether in the destruction of personal relationships or villages and nations, is the outcome of a story of fixed positions and an insoluble conflict. On the other hand, consciously living in the story of an ever-changing relativity generates a fluid, non-resistant relationship with information that challenges existing perception. How one relates to disturbance pivots back to the quality of story developed consciously or otherwise.

There is both beauty and danger in the fact that stories are highly influential and at the same time mutable. Unconscious of attitude, spirit, or operating place, state of being operates at the effect of beliefs that have formed unconsciously, susceptible to the influence of often incomplete, outdated, or originally erroneous meaning. When we are unconscious of the process and lack the skills to adjust the location of attention and thus navigate the course, our faulty stories leave life victim to past descriptions and understandings.

Life ends up on a course as an effect of forces not understood, so one finds oneself in a ship of consciousness that one does not know how to sail, drawing charts that inaccurately reflect the world in which the journey is taking place. With an understanding of the process grounded in essential self, stories develop and update navigational tools, creating usable charts and a successful heading.

Just as the structure of a piece of architecture structures the life that lives within its frame, stories, once created, create the proscenium of the theater of life. The tone of voice of the inner dialogue—the knower (who opens one slit), or the learner (who opens two slits)—sets up the experiment, whether the knower or learner is located by default or consciously positioned. The quality of being, call it spirit or attitude, mood or mindset, or the location of attention, is the lens through which the world is viewed. It is the focus out of which meaning is formed.

Living into the ambiguity leads the unified field experience to merge the comfort of the fixed definitions of classical science with the infinite uncertain potential from the world of quantum mechanics. Through feeling, the aspects of the field experientially recognize their interdependence. A potential hologram of perception appears out of the union.

4

HARMONIZING THE INDIVIDUAL AND THE UNIVERSAL

ENLIGHTENMENT

Spiritual teachings and mystic and esoteric schools commonly refer to enlightenment, awakening, or liberation as a time when the mind opens beyond past conditioning and stories and enters into direct experience of universal energies. Enlightenment, allowing the mystery to express itself, releases us from the imprisonment of the past. It doesn't erase yesterday's understanding or affect the existence or value of patterned and habitual descriptions. As one might take off a jacket coming in from the cold, enlightenment allows one to use the old story when appropriate and set it down when its necessary work is done. The jacket is still there the next time it is needed without having to wear it indoors.

Simply recognizing the process liberates us to some degree. Still, the mind can be captured in struggles of circling thoughts and energies that do not serve the completion of the self. The folktale of Rumpelstiltskin from long ago taught that when under an evil spell, subconsciously magnetized to or held captive by a negative thought or emotional state, the act of naming it, identifying it as a sensation in consciousness, releases the spell and instead allows us to claim its power.

In the psychoanalytic paradigm, taking the repressed energies of subconscious urges and consciously, viscerally accepting these energies (without succumbing to the urges), causes the neuroses to dissolve or seemingly evaporate. In the way of harmonious spirit, conscious experiential presence empowers a story of harmonious creation that manifests fulfillment, an individual's true north, a state of experiencing the unified field of being in the universe. That doesn't mean one loses individuality. The individual and the universal both exist at the same time. Like the poles of a magnetic field they complete each other as one system, a unified field. An individual's central core is the portal and connection to universal conversation. Communication leads to a oneness through the exchange of energies or ideas.

Ki sources the power of development. Absent sufficient power, the unknown looks scary. The monsters and demons of ancient lore and legends were subconscious projections of misunderstandings of the power of the energy rush that we experience in the face of the unknown. With sufficient power, spirit opens into wonder. Experientially activating the power of the central core of aliveness defines the behavior described with the word *courage*, coming from the Latin word that means "of the heart." With the aid of courage, stories serve as stepping stones toward new forms of inquiry. Or, it can just be turtles all the way down.

THE KINGDOM OF HEAVEN

Spiritual quests, religions, and philosophies, as well as every esoteric school in the realm of the spirit, and science in its way, all seek the "kingdom of heaven" in one form or another, in this life or the next. The metaphor of heaven visualizes a harmonious relationship between intent and consciousness, attention and experience, and awareness, enabled by the universal activating principle.

Eastern martial traditions, yoga, the arts, science, religion, and philosophy emanate from a universal calling to bring humanity into harmony with the forces underlying the laws of nature. Unless one path is right and all the others are wrong, a commonality of wisdom can be distilled. The idea of harmony echoes through all philosophies, schools, systems, religions, and sciences, and can be defined as achieving the desired outcome rather than being trapped in conflict, finding peace rather than promoting strife. Instigating all the systems in the realm of the spirit echoes a calling to create a beautiful world in this life, or to teach a way of life that buys a ticket to one in the next.

The many paths up Mount Fuji arrive at the same point. The aspects of life are not separate. They create and are created out of the whole. A path of universal harmony leads religions to completion. Seemingly, whatever religious or scientific position or belief dominates in a culture's story, that story usually includes the promise of benefits or rewards for those who harmonize with the powers or forces that the system identifies.

THE SONG OF THE WIND

Harmony appears in many forms. Moments of inspiring beauty and harmony attune our being into somatic connection with the cosmos. Sometimes, something as simple as slowing down to watch the sunset can return feeling to the experience that, as part of life, one is sustained by the totality of universal forces. Not that anything is said in order to communicate that message. Words don't exist in that space where there is no need for a narrative. Then, later, as all of life's complexities and distractions unfold, that feeling fades into memory. And once forgotten, it often forgets to be re-membered.

As the master said, "calm the spirit; return to source." Each process of letting go of stories allows attention to come back to directly experiencing vitality unmediated, soaking in the beauty of a sunset. Each return to source endows the mystery with the power to reveal itself in the manifest realm. Locating the center of attention in the center of the feeling of aliveness empowers the experience and expression of the mysterious force emanating through self.

Intentionally focusing attention into the experience of enjoying vitality creates harmony and, like any good conversation, warms feelings and strengthens connections between friends. Experientially enjoying the feeling of aliveness, of vitality, increases unification with the universal energy that empowers that vitality. The field of potential takes on a new depth of field, and new synaptic connections proliferate, offering freedom from the known.

Beyond the physical and yet including the physical, beyond anything yet perceived at a conscious level, subtle energies, whisperings of the exalted workings of spirit, offer hints of what it means to experience a state of presence, of power and radiance—a dimensional shift into a superior level of existence. The distractions and challenges of daily life absorb the precious commodity of attention. As a result, one may neither hear, nor as such ever listen to the whisperings in the realm of the spirit, yet they are ever present. And everyone is invited to the conversation.

Whether through a moment of inner quiet, by grace, or by intent, the whisperings may begin to be heard or at first simply vaguely sensed. Often there's a trace of some intangible feeling, unnamable, so subtle it can pass unnoticed. Maybe it's just an odd sense, or a haunting wisp on the threshold of a dream, yet somewhere a whispering surfaces into consciousness; a calling or a sense of mission or destiny beckons, leading toward fulfillment and completion in the best of all possible worlds.

The whisperings of the *Kami*, "divine spirit," show up as subtle feelings. Changes in feeling echo changes in the flow of life energy. The energies of the unified field of mind, body, and spirit harmonize with a situation and crystallize into a flow of guidance. Yet without that knowledge, Ki can feel like disturbance, an upsetting rush of energy, an attacker to be overcome. Absent the power of listening, information that offers the potential to learn will instead collapse, unheard.

The whisperings, present at all times and in all quarters of the universe, make their offering. As the aspects of being come into symphonic attunement, tonalities surface that otherwise function inaccessible to conscious influence. If attention aligns, allowing and appreciating aliveness, the guidance of these tonalities can be felt, understood, and translated into action. In the beginning of the quest, if stillness listens, then aliveness senses the impulse, impetus, and guidance of the energies that are life itself. As the unification of attention with experience attunes, aligning in ever-finer dimensions, a trickle becomes a stream, becomes a river. A whispering becomes a calling.

Feeling, experiencing the glowing aliveness of being, activates unknown powers of the central core. The "spiritual journey" moves the focus of attention, tuning awareness into subtler dimensions and locations that feel better, thus increasing precision alignment between aspects of being. In the finer dimensions of harmony, as the aspects of being entrain, diminishing ambient distraction, the subtle world emerges, stars appear that were never seen before, and answers surface beyond logic and knowledge.

The mysterious whisperings of the exalted workings, the *Mita Hiraki* emanating through the essence of self, speak through the angels of joy and interest. The guidance of the whisperings and the finer dimensions of universal intelligence show up subtly in energy on the horizon of feeling—as images, imagination, and ideas; as an urge, impulse, attraction, or calling; as curiosity; or as echoing whisperings of some fulfillment or destiny yet to unfold.

Experience and expression of universal creative force happen energetically in the hidden realms, and physiologically, hormonally, and somatically in the manifest world. Aliveness feeling, listening experientially to the guidance, brings attention into visceral harmony with creativity, the source of all creation. As the inner dialogue quiets, the known world of history dissolves, and extraordinary facets of the self appear.

Aikido is the study of intent, one of the words used to translate *Ki*. Intent works in mysterious ways beyond imagination. As one of the spooky-weird quantum dualities, intent controls actions, yet it also obeys commands, performing both functions in a back-and-forth process and at the same time. To experientially meld into this superposition is to channel the magic of Aikido. If consciousness is yet to be defined, it is possible intent never will be.

Intent unifies energies, activating and synchronizing whole-being presence. When the aspects of being are in harmony, intelligently aligned, a clear channel exists between individual experience and the creative force of life. A calling and a choice, listening to the subtle forces that inform the manifest realm lights the path of inner wisdom, revealing life's mission and guiding its journey.

ANOTHER LAND

The spiritual journey is the movement of the location of attention. It moves through feeling rather than across distances. The spiritual path, in essence, explores the quality of spirit one is creating and emanating, the quality or state of being out of which the magnetics of life create an individual's reality. Spiritual practice is the study of practices, exercises, and techniques positioning the location or focus of attention. Nadeau Sensei, a direct student of the founder, and with whom I have studied for over fifty years, refers to the basket of technologies that shift state of being as "travel vehicles." Creativity helps those who help themselves. Creative solutions to life's challenges come from positioning attention in one's best operating place.

When a student first begins to respond to the calling of the whisperings, that student goes to the dojo, monastery, ashram, or training hall to learn a different way of being. At first, to let go of the old and take up residence in a new spiritual land requires a different physical location, a separate existence, as is found in these teaching places. To learn a new path or way of being requires, in the beginning of training, going back and forth between the spiritual quest and the demands of life in the manifest realm: one and then the other.

The practice of entering the unknown allows moving freely back and forth between the manifest realm of form, and the divine realm of unformed potential. Going back and forth between an older, established style and a new approach empowers seeing beyond. It helps the student to recognize their growth and development. As training progresses, it becomes possible in the superposition of the quantum world to do both at the same time, to act in the world while relinking, returning to source.

As the two aspects come into harmony, the stories get better. Creative power originates at the source of the internal dialogue, being a part of the creative process rather than reacting to story after it's written. To a limited degree, value lies in techniques that empower, telling a better story. Consciously bridging both realms as one, at the same time, $1 + 1 = 1$ engenders an unfolding field where a better story naturally emerges.

The whispering potential of universal harmony, the field of charm emanating from every subatomic particle, exerts force into the dynamic of creation. In an ongoing state of growth and development, what was once peak performance becomes a standard operating platform, the starting point from which training begins toward a new best operating place. Aikido, like happiness, is not a destination but a way of traveling.

A GREAT LOVE

The power of Aikido works with the energy of change the way a sailor uses the pressure of the wind. A sailor works in harmony with the wind. Even if the winds blow in another direction, because the boat has a keel, a rudder, and the sail is adjustable, someone who understands winds and currents can utilize the forces at play to reach the intended port. Connection to ground keeps life from being blown off course, as a keel does for a ship. Regardless of their direction, a sailor in the spirit of Aiki, grounded in the strong force of central core, adjusting the sail of attention, draws on the power of the winds of change to reach a desired destination to accomplish their bestowed mission.

Relaxation increases connection to ground. Increasing ground connection increases the power of any action, whether the physical ground of earth, or ground of being in the spiritual dimensions. Ground of being will source power to find and follow the path that completes and fulfils the exalted guidance of a given individual. As masculine and feminine unify to create new life, focusing intention into action while letting the whole system relax into grounded connection, gives rise to magic that is only birthed from unification, doing two things at the same time.

A state of imbalance, whether manifested physically, emotionally, or in the realm of thought, will lead energy to naturally seek a return to equilibrium or risk dissipating into the resistance of denial. Imbalance creates a self-perpetuating cycle, where either reaction consumes attention, diminishing access to the neural energy—the Ki of the central core—essential for a creative response to change. As the connection to the pulsating energy that activates and unifies thought and feeling weakens, the breath of creativity wanes. The potential for new synaptic connections follows that curve, leaving story adrift, floating toward a potentially unfulfilling destination.

Feeling somatic connection allows an inner kinesthetic guidance to direct the spiritual journey of attention activating the appropriate areas of the neural system. When the focus of attention is directed to the experience of balance, correction and realignment occur through autonomic guidance. When attention locates focus on one's mission in life, the energy of the universe responds, activating that inquiry. Creativity offers its guidance regardless of whether anyone is listening.

Aiki, cultivating the spirit of reconciliation, blending with the movement of Ki both internally in feeling and externally in action, opens a world beyond fear and aggression, beyond avoiding or resisting. In equal degree, the spirit of attraction becomes increasingly magnetic. The gravity and electromagnetic radiance of aliveness naturally expresses through self as self, attracting the people and experiences that lead one to their true north, toward the fulfillment of their bestowed mission.

Through repeated practice, a spirit of Aiki enters each nanosecond of the unknown anew, in a spirit the founder described as "a great love omnipresent throughout all times and quarters of the universe." Aikido positions attention in the best operating place, as if facing a life-threatening attack—as if every moment were life and death, because cumulatively, that is so.

THE SPHERE OF IMAGINATION

The reciprocating echoes of stories and perception both develop from and impart meaning to experience. Perception, whether accurate, inferred, or imagined, is relative and determined by point of view. Internally, the location of the focus of attention affects the inner world of experience, attitude, affect, and the mental, emotional, and spiritual dimensions of being. Even the subtlest shift in the location of the internal realms of thought, imagination, muscle tone, or emotional affect will alter the focus and frame of reference. Perception and understanding of the universe will change in tandem.

Everything looks different seen through a different window. This phenomenon is beautifully exemplified in Akira Kurosawa's film *Rashomon*, the story of an event told from several different perspectives. When each participant translates their experience into their story or description of what happened, the stories have almost no relationship to one another. The geocentric perception that the sun goes around the Earth seems observably true from a relative position on the surface of the planet. The universe looks different from outer space.

Perception is relative to perspective. Emotionality is a filter that colors the meaning made from perspective. An issue causing upset at one point in time might be laughed off at another, relative to the degree of inner harmony and free energy present. Through one window, the realm of emotional experience can be conceptualized as a location on a continuum, from feeling great on one end to terrible on the other.

LOCATION: THE ENERGY CONTINUUM

On one end of the continuum, we live feeling the glow of life with the pure joy of an infant. On the other, under pressure from the same life energy, stress becomes distress.

With the recognition of the relativity of location and its effect on perception and story, the process of story becomes mutable. The location of attention surfaces into conscious awareness and can be named, opening the possibility of positioning attention with intent—putting attention in the driver's seat.

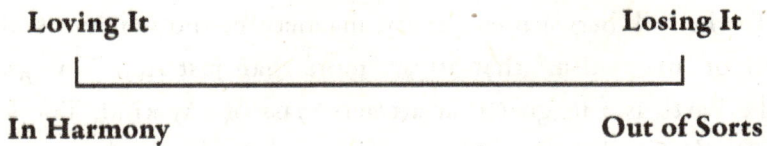

Loving It   **Losing It**

In Harmony   **Out of Sorts**

Adjusting attention's relative position has a transformative impact, shaping reciprocating echoes that extend across a vast interplay of forces. The ability to position attention, to locate the focus of experience in a quality, a chosen spirit, an attitude, or a way of being is a developable skill. The ability to locate and reposition attention, thus affecting quality of experience, progresses like any skill, through intentional practice and repetition.

ELECTRICITY, MAGNETISM, AND GRAVITY

Every life form generates a magnetic field that affects and is affected by everything else in the universe. The field, in turn, magnetically attracts some people or things and repels others. As the universal force strengthens, as more Ki flows through the system, the power of the spirit of attraction is cultivated and becomes stronger, increasing the curvature of time-space, changing the reality of life. These are the reciprocating echoes of the universal Ki.

Wrapping a wire around a nail and running an electric current through the wire creates an electromagnet. The flow of electrons around an iron core aligns the polarities of its molecules, creating a magnetic field. Increase the flow of electricity, and the magnet becomes stronger. Diminish the current and the magnetic field weakens. Similarly, when the battery in a flashlight or a portable tape recorder is running down, it diminishes the level of light or slows the tape.

All the functions of the human system run on energy. When there is sufficient energy, they work efficiently. When they lack sufficient energy, compensatory behavior struggles with the deficit, potentially leading to a breakdown. Too much energy and the system overloads, burning up or burning out.

In the link between electricity, magnetism, and gravity, there are forces of "magnetism" that attract more than just iron. The gravity of the Earth is a magnet that attracts mass of any kind. The moon attracts the Earth, relative to its mass, much as the Earth attracts the moon. The gravitational force of a planet pulls on the space around it. Ki connects a universal field between subatomic particles and galaxies, a convergence of inexplicable mystery.

People, as emotional magnets, generate a quality of magnetism, generally without the awareness of doing so, and without knowing how powerfully it affects life. The aliveness of being broadcasts a radiant glow into the world through the bio-electromagnetic field, as well as a magnetism of gravity. The gravitational field of the spirit of attraction magnetically materializes everything in the sphere of the subtle force, coloring the quality of experience.

Each shift in feeling into the central core of life energy changes the field of potential. Tensing or relaxing muscle tone brings forth a different feeling, or a different stance, affect, or emotional tone in the world. The tonality of feeling radiates a bio-electromagnetic resonance of the self. The filters of affect and thought color it.

When the aspects of being come into symphonic resonance, experience changes, like going through a time warp or portal into another dimension. Every breakthrough in sports, creativity, or thinking is an expression of this phenomenon. Osensei showed hints of the larger implications of what might be possible. As a dimensional shift unfolds, limitations that used to exist dissolve. Powers previously unknown appear. Any master musician, artist, or athlete has some degree of awareness of the process and recognizes this experience.

The degree of precision of attention's position can be fine-tuned. Aligning proper relationship with Ki is an exploration into the quality of spirit that flows through the magnetic coil of life. In the beginning, tuning the magnetic field may seem a very subtle tonality. Yet with attention, it becomes tangible. With practice, intent becomes an art.

THOUGHT AND ACTION,
KARMA AND DESTINY

The startle effect from a sudden rush of aliveness potentially pushes attention from feeling experientially into focusing instead on stories describing experience. The areas of the brain attending to and activating visceral sensation diminish, withdrawing awareness from feeling. Unpleasant stories especially, and even pleasant ones, give birth to extensive rumination. Memories from incomplete experience can go back decades and still disturb brain wave patterns and drain attention.

Calming the spirit, returning to source, attention opens into the power of the central core. The electromagnetic radiance of the central core increases in force closer to center. In the increasing radiance, attention can feel pushed out of central core as the waves push back when we walk into the ocean.

The intensity of the pressure of energy increases on approach into the experience of self. The centrifugal forces intensify the closer the center of attention gets to the center of the radiance of Ki, the experience of vitality. As these forces radiate outward with ever-increasing intensity on approach, the message is not "avoid the energy" or "don't meditate." The message is that attention and experience have some singing practice to do.

As attention positions itself closer to the central core of being, each adjustment in alignment of attention toward the center of the central core gets decidedly smaller and the shift subtler as the radiant outward force increases. As the radiance of energy is stronger, pushing attention into discomfort, the likelihood of failing to notice the finer adjustments, or of undervaluing their importance, increases. Yet as the fine-tuning gets finer, each movement "in" has exponentially greater effect on the magnetic field and level of power emanating. The effect is remarkable relative to the subtlety of each finer movement of the spiritual journey.

Presence accesses the energy of the central core, inhaling its power. As we unify and harmonize, absorb the activation, imbibe Ki, eat the energy, the glow of the field of potential increases. The power absorbed enables repositioning at each instant with positive intent. When peaceful reconciliation creates a field of acceptance, releasing dissonance with the past, all energy empowers entry into the future in a positive and coherent spirit. A warrior enters into feeling, changing discomfort into Aiki and conflict into confluence, and contributing a harmonious tonality to the world.

A ship at sea or a plane in flight adjusts course ceaselessly until it reaches its intended destination. A change in the field of potential through something as subtle as feeling differently produces a different story, though all other aspects may remain the same. With a slight change in story, life on a new tack ends up in a different world. Adjusting the course of life, consciously adjusting attitude and temperament with every breath, takes one home.

The importance of generating a seed crystal of positive, reciprocating echoes at the inception of any engagement cannot be overstated. This is true whether we are beginning an important negotiation or simply setting the quality of spirit as we start each new day, like key codes aligned at the hint of dawn to inform the software programs of life.

Aligning with the force of creation, even an approach on feeling into the totality, changes experience, increasing confidence, comfort, enhanced personal strength, and vitality. Through activating the field by increasing the awareness and balance of center and circle, possibilities increase. Balance all four forces, and the field of potential increases exponentially. Spiritual practices that tune the aspects of being into symphonic resonance can transform the quality of vibration, where thought and action, karma and destiny originate.

ACCENTUATE THE POSITIVE

Under the light of attention, the potential of choice enters the conscious realm. Choosing to think positive thoughts about things that bring joy locates awareness, activating the somatic network with a quality of feeling that resonates throughout the system of aliveness. Letting attention be taken by insistent feelings of vexation activates different neural patterns and alters somatic experience. Once established, whether intentionally or otherwise, the quality of attitude, affect, or spirit generated becomes the seed crystal and fundamental tone in subsequent interactions. The magic of Aikido trains us to choose to reposition attention in a spirit of harmonious relationship with Ki, regardless of the challenge.

Place a magnet near a bar of iron and the iron will magnetize, meaning the polarity of the molecules of iron will align magnetically with the north and south poles of the magnetic field encompassing it. The increased coherence of molecular alignment, in a back-and-forth process, is produced by and produces a magnetic field. The iron bar becomes a magnet under the influence of a larger magnetic field. Take the magnet away, and gradually the magnetic alignment of the molecules making up the bar of iron will degrade back to the original random state, losing the magnetic force.

Learning to go into and through the initial sense of disturbance, and change the story from one of discomfort to develop a radiant new state of being, is fundamentally simple and easy. It is as simple as feeling better intentionally. A deep breath, a fond memory, and even the simple act of feeling into the experience of the moment, are all travel vehicles for the spiritual journey. With the aid of these vehicles, the shift into feeling better is not only simple and easy, it takes no more than a second.

The challenge is establishing it as a new fundamental base level. Problematically, the gravity of habituation continues to de-magnetize attention back toward previous familiar locations, levels of tension, and boundaries of capability. To keep the power from degrading, a challenging degree of focused repetition is required until a better operating place becomes the central position.

Positioning really means *repositioning* because the relative field of continual change requires constantly readjusting with every pulse of universal energy. Realignment to staying on course is an ongoing act of repositioning, grounding, returning to source, and appreciating the downward-sinking force while enjoying the rush of activation. From the simplest skills to the most sophisticated art, mastery develops in the forge of training.

Facing the uncertainty of potential death in the next engagement, a warrior trains, enhancing their power to position attention. Repositioning attention into the center of the central core, when practiced religiously through repetition, gives birth to a new ground of being. Gradually a state of greater Aiki begins to feel familiar, like home, and becomes the new starting point for today's training.

A permanent magnet is created by placing iron in a magnetic field and putting the iron molecules under pressure. In the world of training, that means repetition and focus, time and energy. Practice in simply "feeling better" develops a reinforcing cycle, so that "even by drops the bucket is filled." Transforming what is possible, imagination introduces synaptic patterns in a dimension beyond any that logic and reason can access. Training beyond the norm magnetizes results beyond the norm. Life takes on a quality that seems miraculous to someone living in a "mind of discord."

The journey into alignment of self with the whole of creation begins with the single step of focusing attention into experiential appreciation of the Ki of the central core. Inhaling, absorbing, or unifying with the energy is fundamental. Inspiration, in both the physical and energetic realms, is the fuel transporting spirit on its journey. The increasing possibility can be felt in the resonance of the breath with the pulse of life energy. When personal Ki finds unity with the energy that sources creation, capability and possibility open the imagination.

The wind can be felt, but it is seen through the movement of the leaves. Ki moves unseen, but like the wind it can be felt through the energy on the move in the alive system. It shows up in the physical realm as reactivity, neural pulses, synaptic exchange, and the overall glow of energy that radiates through the hologram of neurology. In the same way that the movement of the leaves makes the wind visible, and physiology or reactivity makes Ki visible, the magic of imagination expresses the power of creativity.

Feeling induces coherence, unifying the field. Every pulse of attention, feeling into connection with vitality, is a micro-dose of meditation. Listening to whisperings of feeling allows the natural entrainment of forces. When connected to ground of being, a relationship of greater harmony functions with the power of a laser, as opposed to incoherent light that illuminates but does not produce action or induce change.

Attention, focusing into experiencing Ki, aligns and balances the four forces. The field of unification guides the development of an increasingly coherent, personally aligned intelligence. An exalted field of intelligence serves as a powerful internal compass that directs life.

PURE AND ORIGINAL SELF: THE HIDDEN AND DIVINE REALMS

In the lexicon of psychology, the self describes an amalgam of the aspects of consciousness. Commonly, the word *self* has been used to distinguish an individual from everything else, with the self understood as separate. In postmodern usage, the word *self* has devolved and come to be used somewhat interchangeably with the term *ego*. The dictionary compounds the confusion by calling the ego the "I" or self. *Ego* comes out of ancient Greek mythology implying "one who has stopped listening to the gods."

Psychology defines the ego as the part of the psyche balancing self-fulfillment and self-esteem between the primitive drives of the id and the demands of the social environment, represented by the superego. *Ego* is the English word commonly used in modern translation of the Sanskrit term *Ahamkara* (*aham*, "self" – *kara*, "doer") though here again in identifying the separateness, this definition misses the unity implied in the original concept. In yogic teachings, *Ahamkara* describes "the consciousness principle" that raises human consciousness above the realm of the animals while limiting its entry to the realm of the gods.

From the perspective of Aikido, all the above descriptions refer to manifestations of the self, the dust after the action. The word *ego* and the word *self* define different facets of the potential field of being. *Ego* points to the identification that separates. *Self*, which includes and yet exceeds the intellect and id, evokes the portal of connection. The Sanskrit term *atman*, describing the aliveness of universal spirit in pure manifestation through an individual, resonates with quantum implications of the term *self*.

In the teachings of yoga, the source of human suffering is mis-identification of identity as the self. Albert Einstein is thought to have said, "The greatest tragedy of human existence is the illusion of separateness." The founder of Aikido said similarly, "Problems of the world exist because people have forgotten that everything emanates from a single source."

The sense of an individual self as separate and distinct, while valid in the world of classical science, fails to reconcile fixed understanding and belief with the confusing, entangled world of the quantum story, where everything is connected to everything in a unified field. In the quantum world, the mirage of self exists as energetic potential in a field of uncertainty. In interaction back and forth, energetic potential collapses into identity, character, and persona. Depending on the focus of attention, these either become fixed or dissolve back into the field of potential in the quiet, downward-sinking release of returning to source.

The flow of life enters the unknown. The forks in the road require decisive action. Though neither the classical nor the quantum story describes creation accurately, both serve their functions. Going back and forth between the two suspends consciousness over the chasm, gazing into the vastness of an incomprehensible mystery. Learning to enjoy, explore, and feel an active part of that mystery is the purpose and power of a spiritual warrior's training.

KNOW THYSELF

The primary directive to "know thyself" poses the core question, "Who am I?" Concepts like "finding one's self," or one's "true north," or knowing what to do when there is no clear path, all stem from a fundamental yearning to reconcile with the world. Reconciliation means allowing the completion of life's mission, to do what is right and to arrive at the right destination having done the right things. Accuracy, seemingly valuable in the abstract, only matters in the value of story to the degree that it serves function.

The proverbial journey in search of the self echoes across all cultures, ages, and geographies, to the point that it has become almost a cliché. At the same time, most people cannot simply sit quietly with themselves for more than a moment without feeling uncomfortable. Discomfort implies not feeling harmoniously connected with strength, forte, or Ki—the source of power, whether personal or divine.

The rush of energy surges, activating the alive system with the intention of being of service. In empowering action, it disturbs the status quo. The first common reaction to disturbance in any form is to be startled—although we only refer to the reaction that way when it is substantial. Yet even the millions of smaller rushes that go unnoticed echo the same fundamental process.

Once stimulated, the system goes on alert to detect the cause. This is the bifurcation point where, potentially, one story might ask if something is wrong. Out of that field of potential, once story reacts to disturbance and describes it as discomfort, looking to explain the "problem," a decision has already been taken, and the fork in the road has already been chosen. Down this path the disturbance, the rush of energy, comes to be described as an experience to be avoided or controlled. This dissonance magnetically repulses attention away from the central core, the rush, the flow of Ki.

The word *discomfort* means moving away from the power needed to create the desired change. The need for change is indicated by the disturbing energy signal labeled *discomfort*. Yet this movement away from the experience of disturbance is the actual discomfort. *Discomfort* describes moving away from being with strength (*dis*, "to move away from," as in dismount or disconnect; *com*, "with"; and *forte*, "strength").

Discomfort signals moving away from the power of vitality. Creativity means connecting with it, listening to the message. Whether the energy enhances our ability to produce an exceptional performance or, at the other end of the continuum, debilitates us, depends very much on the quality of alignment between the aspects of being, whether one has "found one's self."

COM FORTE: WITH STRENGTH

Comfortable translates into "ability with strength." The less free energy available, the more threatening any change, incoming energy, or information may seem, whether it truly is or not. Denial, resistance, and avoidance all absorb precious attention required to process the disturbance created by new information. When comfortable in spirit, story, instead of asking what is wrong, could be written from a state of confidence to ask what is *changing*, thus setting in motion a different set of reciprocating echoes and creating a different universe. As a first teaching, Aikido means training to align relationship with the energy as an empowering partner in a process, as a positive force to be understood and worked with in a spirit of harmony.

Inquiry and knowledge, pure science and applied science, translate in the art of Aikido as "blend and lead." When the rush surges, the reactive tendency is to lead first without blending, to try to change the situation without sufficiently comprehending it. Then the universe is out of order, out of harmony. Getting centered, locating a best operating place, is step one. Listening is step two. Listening does not actually occur until something changes in the listener. Only then is it possible to know whether one should speak or not, and if so, the appropriate thing to say.

From a mindset of living in the inner tension of duality, getting comfortable may be understood as just relaxing. In the way of harmony, getting comfortable, harmonizing with the energy, is more than the relaxation aspect, releasing to the downward-sinking force. Equally important for the manifestation of spirit is appreciation and enjoyment of the vitality of the upward-rising force, the radiant glow of increasing energy.

Being with the strength means equally enjoying the pleasure of relaxation and the vitality of the rush—both at the same time. To be comfortable is to harmonize with the energy to achieve the perfect tone for a given situation, instant by instant. Comfort, moving "into and with" strength, manifests the power that originates out of the source of creation and unfolds into a fulfilling life. Balancing the exact right degree of tension and relaxation, of back-and-forth comprehending and strategizing, manifests the hidden powers of the central core and the enjoyment of universal energy.

In an energy universe, the term *self* depicts an experiential portal unifying individual with universal Ki. Original self represents the glowing, vital, animating principle of being, the universal spirit appearing through an individual hologram. As the dross burns away, true self, original self, the experiential aliveness of being, naturally expresses dynamic interconnection with universal: $1 + 1 = 1$. Cosmic consciousness emerges, a felt sense of aliveness and universal interconnection.

One story defaults to avoiding the discomfort of disturbance, thereby increasing fragmentation. Another, the story out of Aikiland, aligns with the signals of the changing energy, listening to the whisperings. Following the guidance of the energy into harmonious relationship intones the unified field experience. Self-sacrifice, in the dimensional shift of Aikido, surrenders the known self to the next dimension of consciousness.

In every dimension, the twin forces seek harmony, expressing the natural creativity of universal Ki. As the aspects align, the channel opens in resonance. Creativity, the unfolding aspiration of the universe, comes forth. Permeating feeling and thought, entering any space or opening, the flowing creative mystery gives birth to unimagined connections, processes, and outcomes. Standing on the floating bridge of heaven, being in the manifest known and the divine unknown at the same time and in the same time-space, generates a field of awareness through which the creativity of the universe is always manifesting, always expressing.

Ongoing development in intergalactic astronomy continues to

advance cosmology, each answer posing larger questions. As study deepens into the subatomic realm, the quantum universe becomes even spookier. In a similar way, exploration into the self should come with a warning: "finding one's self" doesn't arrive at a fixed point.

Self is not a thing. Self, as an interface, opens a timeless inquiry into the mystery through which creativity activates, thus enhancing ability to surmount the challenges each moment offers. Entrance into the mystery happens through feeling into the central core at each moment, because "experiential self" is the magic theater.

DRAGONS GUARD THE TEMPLE

When the creativity of Ki starts to flow, limited identity, standing guard at the door in a reactive story of self-protection, opposes change instead of allowing the energy of the moment to redefine the moment. A narrow path leads to direct experience, re-visioning the energy called discomfort or fear into what in Buddhist terminology is referred to as *sunyata*, the shining void, and in the quantum domain as the *field of potential*. Discomfort, before it became a story, before being observed and named, was feeling, change, disturbance. It was information flowing as energy, guidance, a message, a whispering.

Before it is called discomfort, disturbance caused by the energy rush is simply energy on the move, the alive system activating reset, responding to change. The feeling of discomfort is a signal of awareness, warning attention of the potential danger of moving away from the energy that is the source of its power.

Flinching is a hardwired response. Reactivity has been practicing its story for eons. In the reversed imagery of the mirror of consciousness, wanting to move away from the sense of dis-comfort means moving into the power of the source of disturbance. Going toward and into the discomfort is what turns it into comfort, or being with strength. One moves out of discomfort in this quantum through-the-looking-glass world by entering into it.

In Aikido, one enters "off the line," in a spirit of inquiry, not opposition. Opening to the energies, assimilating the guidance, and listening—these are all acts of courage. Entering new levels of energy may not feel comfortable at first. As when we get into a hot bath, it may take a minute to adjust before the system allows itself to open, settle, and enjoy. Reactivity wants to withdraw from the experience. A thalamic pause, not accepting the first feeling as the definitive message, facilitates the transition from a reactive to a more considered response.

Courage is neither denying the impulse of energy nor resisting it. Courage is acting intelligently and harmoniously in relationship to the energy that, when resisted, sources the feeling commonly called fear. Courage implies a story-framing state of mind that serves the completion of a challenge, task, or mission. The way of harmony implies "eating the energy," inhaling, absorbing, and assimilating it, and applying the potential energy "a second before" it is called fear, utilizing it as a call to action, a source of power.

The intent of the system stimulating the rush is to complete the mission assigned in response to any change. The message of the energy rush, when resisted in a misunderstanding or mistranslation of discomfort, results in pushing attention further from the source, in opposition to the energy's intent. Listening to the original intent, or "eating the energy," returns attention to the vitality of the unified field experience, in the spirit of a great love.

TEMPERING THE SWORD
OF ENGAGEMENT

I feel what you feel that you call fear but I called it a call to action.

OSENSEI

Fear is the harbinger of power.

NADEAU SENSEI

Temperament is a cornerstone of intellect, as the value and capability of a sword's edge is based on its temper. A sword is tempered in the forge, going back and forth between the exact right degree of heat and cold, each for the exact right amount of time, to produce precision balance of hardness without brittleness, strength with resilience.

Temperament describes the cumulative outcome or long-term effects of the quality of being called *mood*, also called *humor* in an earlier usage. When we are in poor humor, every criticism gives offense. On a good day, when we are properly aligned with strength, comfortable, it doesn't. If one is improperly aligned, criticism, instead of being received as guidance, is heard only as an insult or attack. When one lacks comfort in one's inner world, the messages of Ki are reacted to in a similar negative vein. If all criticism or guidance is taken through that frame, the potential value of such feedback gets lost, as does the energy wasted resisting it.

Some people give well-worded criticism, making it easy to receive. Some people seem to deliver criticism as an attack. But this distinction doesn't matter. In the study of Aikido, the practice develops listening to the message, not the tonality. Aikido aligns relationship with the input, energy, or information at its source, dealing with the essential issue. Once the energy is identified and unified, the spirit of reconciliation returns it to the field of potential, making it available to be used for positive outcomes.

When one is in a bad mood, failing to clearly consider or appropriately value criteria, decisions are made reactively, impulsively. In a phase of diminishing connection to source of power, every pressure stresses the body, weakens the immune system, blocks thinking, stifles creativity, and inevitably leads to failing to prioritize the choices in life that really matter at an appropriate level. Instead one overvalues choices that don't actually affect one's life very much. Connection to the central core allows decisions to be made accordingly, in alignment with one's true north or bestowed mission.

It looks like the sun goes around the Earth. From inside an

experience, once attention is captured by mood, that experience feels like reality, universal truth. Discomfort is a request for acknowledgment. To quote Proverbs 3:6, "In all thy ways acknowledge him, and he shall direct thy paths." Acknowledgment indicates listening to the energy's message. Without sufficient awareness of that message guiding our return to source, and listening instead to the message of discomfort guiding return to source, attention continues to operate out of sorts. When temper is lost, self-awareness and self-reflexivity seem to go out the same window at the same time, because they exist in an interconnected field of quantum entanglement.

In a good mood, an insult can be laughed off, criticism received well, and any positive information put to good use. A positive state of mind, maintaining positive Ki, makes the difference between casting oneself as a victim versus telling a good story of positive spirit that accesses creativity.

External forces, thoughts, and memories affect mood, and mood, without the gift of Aikido, is easily tempered by the magnetism or gravity of a situation. Most children know there are better and worse times to ask their parents for something. And everyone knows that when someone is in a bad mood, it is not the best time to have a talk with them. Human behavior commonly responds in kind to experienced behavior, or more accurately, to the story about the experience. A second before a decision collapses the infinite field, the power of a harmonious spirit is immeasurably valuable in creating a better story.

Training, or changing state, opens the field of potential of attuning mood, enabling a state of feeling better intentionally. When the possibility to choose "a good day" is implemented, a better story emerges. Rather than living at the mercy of the evolution of brain structure and events in a field of potential uncertainty, it is possible to pay attention to developing self-reflexivity and to buy conscious choice regarding temperament.

When we are thrown off by the intensity of a rush, healing requires conscious attention and a process of correcting alignment. Otherwise, overwhelm increases in a vicious cycle. All of this affects and is affected by mood, attitude, and state of being. Mood sustained over time accumulates, solidifying into temperament. Temperament, with its mood du jour overlay, colors experiences and affects meaning and the basis of thought and strategy, as well as the transmission of every communication.

Though being in a bad mood can cause serious problems, the problem is not mood. Mood is mutable. The problem is mistakenly identifying with a passing feeling as if that were the self. Story sets up an experiment: to see through one slit, identifying *as* the anger, versus through two slits, creating a story about awareness of *feeling* anger. These stories unfold different universes. However, unless the internal conversation that writes the story receives active attention, the potential field of choice collapses, left unexercised.

The first step to being in a better mood begins with intent, refining the quality and degree of self-reflexivity. Feeling better, feeling into experience more consciously, develops the system's response ability, allowing it to clearly receive the guidance of the inner signals and position attention in a location that feels better. Intentionally valuing somatic tonalities and letting affect surface into consciousness enables the birthing of mood out of intent.

SELF-REFLEXIVITY

Attention's location or operating place, where someone is coming from, selects what will be looked at and colors how it will be looked at. As the eye cannot see itself, as the tongue cannot taste itself, state of being generally operates without awareness of its influence. This challenge is exacerbated in a rush of energy. As reactivity increases when unattended, awareness diminishes in equal proportion. In the heat of action in an intense situation, without the power of self-reflexivity, signals are missed and the system fails to effectively self-correct.

Reflectivity implies the seeing eye of awareness. Reflexivity means adaptability to stimulus or perception. Flowers are both reflective and reflexive. They not only reflectively sense where the sun is, they reflexively turn toward it.

When we "lose it"—"it" being self-reflexivity—and go off on someone or about something, the outburst feels good in the moment, in that it allows energy to flow. Yet being "out of it," being emotionally abusive or irrational, implies an inability to read the signals. As the container shatters, the energy pressure releases. However, the Ki is destructive.

The degree of questionable behavior indicates the degree of loss of balance in center-circle connection. When we develop sensitivity that lets us hear and read the signals, alarm bells ring at the first sign of self-righteousness. Without awareness of the process, when reactivity disturbs attention's connection, the reverse happens.

Self-reflexivity implies recognizing the first signs of losing it, and acknowledging irrational behavior early enough to change the course of action before it's too late. Whether for executing a martial technique, responding appropriately in an emergency on the freeway, or getting into a heated argument, the art offers the same guidance: calm the spirit and return the focus of attention to the center of the source, the feeling of aliveness.

As conversations or situations flare up, self-reflexivity diminishes. The training focuses on intentionally activating the shift into circle-center balance a second before the attack takes form, or a second before one says something that can never be taken back. In a crisis, spirit's primary directive is to create the most coherent state from which to originate function.

Self-reflexivity, though it can be somewhat elusive, is relatively easy in the physical domain where the signals are tangible. Once training develops the knowledge and attention to look for the signals and alarms, checking the instruments and understanding the signals is not hard. Emotional and attitudinal issues and signs are considerably subtler than the physical, but still readable if one learns to read.

Self-reflexivity in the mental domain is a challenge because a developing belief system carves and repeatedly reestablishes neural and synaptic pathways. Patterns become so ingrained that they disappear from conscious awareness and therefore conscious influence. Thought defensively entrenches itself as attention drifts further from connection to central core. The repetition and reinforcement make it increasingly difficult for attention to recognize and reorganize the process.

This is a situation where temperament is more important than intellect. Sadly, the smarter a person is, the better they can be at convincing themselves of what they already believe. Temper is fundamental to the value of a sword's edge. Unless a clear intention is forged to dissolve fixation on the past, challenge established beliefs, and open to the future, thought patterns reinforce themselves, channeling energy into established synaptic grooves, into the sunset.

Feeling is always available to offer guidance. The total field of being informs thinking/feeling vitality, naturally and seemingly effortlessly, when allowed to do so. However, physical, mental, and emotional habituation, as well as resistance in the system, impede this natural process. Though liberation can happen spontaneously, to enter the unknown intentionally, opening to new ways of looking, usually requires the energy of intent.

When seen from a viewpoint that does not encompass the whole, "reality" is a perspective. This truth should be easy to see, but for all the reasons this study addresses, it doesn't seem to be—at least, as the Bible points out, not as easy as seeing the incoherence in other people's thinking: "Why do you see the speck in your neighbor's eye, but do not notice the log in your own eye? . . . You hypocrite, first take the log out of your own eye, and then you will see clearly to take the speck out of your neighbor's eye" (Matthew 7:3–5).

Waking up to the fact that we've drifted out of the correct lane requires an intentional interest in recognizing signals reflexively. Cultivating the spirit of reconciliation, a spirit of listening and harmony, takes courage and personal power, free energy. The process rewards in more than equal measure.

The totality of the alive system comprehends complexity and plots out behaviors, direction, and action beyond what is possible out of the known. Then realms beyond the conscious divine a path, a way to attain the appropriate destination. Creativity emerges in service of accomplishing one's bestowed mission.

Self-reflexivity can be like the instrument panel and controls that allow a pilot to fly an airplane when visibility is less than optimal. A spirit of harmony trains gratefully, learning to notice signs of disturbance or discomfort, because it is feeling into the experience of disturbance that supplies the energy (read: information) that guides correction.

Feeling locates attention in the driver seat. Thinking maps the journey, while feeling drives the car. Conscious attention to experience makes it possible to choose a path and reach a desired destination. Feeling energy gives birth to movement, creating the dance of life in harmony with universal rhythms.

FORGING A WARRIOR'S TEMPERAMENT

Warrior training actualizes presence and refines precision in focus of attention. A warrior forges intent, blending the energies of the dual forces—fire, or upward rising, and water, or downward sinking—producing fluid adaptability with laser intensity. Everything is affected. In the beginning of developing the unified field experience as baseline, attention goes back and forth from the heat and intensity of the central core to the coolness of space and the relationships of life, each in their orbits. Through intent, the focus of attention develops a balanced relationship between the forces, and a spirit of harmony is tempered.

Aiki is technology for transforming life. When it comes to consciously tempering the spirit that one lives in, as in every study there are fundamental skills, techniques, and understandings that facilitate proficiency. Standing on the floating bridge of heaven that Aiki requires to come forth means moving awareness into experience, bridging harmonious relationship of self with universal Ki. The ongoing return of attention to intentionally, experientially aligning center with the mystery is the fundamental transformational practice from which everything else flows. The unified field experience exists simply as potential until activated by intent.

Focusing attention on unifying the aspects of being is not done in thought, it emanates out of feeling. Feeling, as humble as it may seem, reconciles attention and vitality, mind and body. Soma is the unifying link between psyche and corpus. The power to influence mood grows out of experientially balancing the electromagnetic and gravitational forces with the central core and the subtle force.

Being present, moving in harmonious relationship with the force of an attack, neutralizes the threat. Transforming the intent or force of the attack into free energy opens the possibility of returning energy to the field of potential. The principle applies equally to transforming internal energy. Attention, in harmonious relationship with the mysterious cosmic force of change, transforms the story of conflict into one of confluence, enhancing the field out of which kaleidoscopic possibilities for reconciliation issue forth.

The power of harmony starts with correcting the discord in one's own mind. In a centered and grounded state, energy flows from its nature, creativity. The reciprocating echoes of the mood of spirit radiate outward into the life of an individual, and the tone of society, a collection of individuals. The alive system, glowing in a state of presence, enters the circle of life facing each challenge creatively. Creativity fixes the problem, not the blame.

Story makes meaning, and by doing so, decides whether life is lived in a positive spirit or in some other quality. Knowledge only has value to the degree that it enriches experiential reality. The location of attention, like the sail, is adjustable. It is the point of leverage and the source of power with which to navigate the ocean of life, amidst the winds of change. Aikido sees state as mutable and best operating place as life-and-death critical, regardless of the time that one imagines one has remaining.

Harmony within produces harmony without. The magic mirror

reflects in the outer world the quality of the internal relationship of attention and vitality. The founder frequently referred to standing on the floating bridge of heaven. He repeatedly emphasized that a state of being unifying the two forces into one, $1 + 1 = 1$, was necessary for Aiki to come forth. Without that, all the technical practice would produce the equivalent of a sword that is not properly tempered.

FIXING THE PROBLEM

It's difficult to enjoy time with a couple who are always arguing, continually being rude and insulting toward each other. It is difficult to find dinner companions for a couple who radiate that quality of disagreement. Similarly, no one wants to go to dinner with someone whose internal masculine and feminine forces are in constant conflict. Everyone is made up of a mother and father and has within them masculine and feminine qualities, yin and yang, thought and feeling, mind and body, sensitivity and strength. When the forces are out of balance or in conflict with each other, they radiate dissonance and repel attention, producing the opposite of the spirit of attraction.

Emotional electromagnetism moves away from someone who is exhibiting a dissonant, frustrated, or angry affect. Even simply being alone won't be enjoyable when the internal aspects of being are not in harmony. It is difficult to enjoy being with someone who is not enjoying their own experience, especially if that person is oneself.

Consciously or otherwise, the degree of inner harmony or dissonance colors everything felt and communicated, attracted and repelled. The reciprocating echoes sent out are usually done so unconsciously. Energy sent forth in a positive spirit of harmony and reconciliation engenders a resonant quality. Attuning consciousness increases in value in the hidden realm where it is less visible. Unseen power lies in attending to the quality of the inner dialogue, the voice with which one speaks to oneself. It sets the tone of the electromagnetic radiance projected into the world.

The dissonance between internal aspects of being contributes to both why it's difficult to sit alone and why people can have such difficulty getting along with each other. Harmony won't be achieved with another when one's internal aspects are busy channeling creative force into an internal argument. Singing off key contributes the opposite of harmony. Unless mood and temperament correct themselves, even the singers will not want to attend the performance.

Everyone deals with the same issue, so unless it is corrected, when people come together the off-center vibrations of two people reinforce each other, amplifying the problem. When the masculine and feminine forces of the universe engage in dialogue, within an individual or between individuals, the differences vibrate in a dynamic tension that births peaceful reconciliation within and without.

Attention experiences reality and creates meaning and stories as heavily influenced by state, mood, and temperament as by past patterning. The reciprocating echoes dramatically affect the unfolding experience. The way of harmony is the art of creating state of being as a source of power. Aikido, by consciously forming a warrior temperament, develops in us the ability to select and influence the location of attention, mood, or attitude.

The physiological impulses of neural energy are driven by finer energies that activate the unfolding, manifest world. As a musician develops their ear to produce a finer sensibility, repositioning allows the fine-tuning of temperament constantly and precisely, in relationship to the flow of life. Aikido dims the ambient light of thoughts and belief systems and manifests perception in a finer dimension, thus perceiving a different and richer reality. The previously invisible stars that appear out of the darkness enable the navigator to adjust and realign temperament as an intentional, generative tone. As we feel into presence, each moment realigns, creating a constant precision alignment to a universe of continual change.

A single instance of attending to or disregarding mood may not seem that important, but string together many such instances and they become the destiny of a life. Surfacing mood into experiential awareness raises it out of the captive influence of the default mode network. Intentionally choosing a mood that's enjoyable develops a conscious set of synaptic pathways that write a better story, to the benefit of everyone involved, both the practitioner and, and to some degree, everyone in their life.

BEYOND IDENTITY:
THE IDENTITY'S DILEMMA

Repeating familiar ways of thinking and feeling habituates developing a persona, a style, a character. Identification sets up the quality of one's relationship with the energy of the universe. As mood becomes temperament, temperament becomes character. Character, repeated sufficiently, essentially becomes identity. Over time, identity calcifies. When a branch is growing and green, it is easily guided. As it hardens into wood, that possibility diminishes.

When change demands action beyond identity's comfort zone, creativity offers energies that transcend identity. In response to any situation where energy flow increases, if identity—the size of the channel—stays the same, pressure on the system increases. Opening, releasing the boundaries of identity, allows a shift, an adjustment of identity to new parameters. The phrase "be big about it" means seeing the bigger picture, allowing energy the size of conduit that it needs. Just as we change the clothes on our body as we grow, the self changes identities as it develops. Self is not an identity but rather a dynamic portal bridging dimensions.

Identity is a tool of interaction. As identity falls into believing itself, it loses the vital connection to the central core in a self-fulfilling process. Lack of power produces a state of anxiety that grows into fear. Lacking conscious intent, identifying as identity, life defaults down established synaptic pathways of increasing defensiveness. The shift into presence, by contrast, intentionally develops the path of increasing connection to the universe. In a state of confidence, or comfort aligned with power, identity recognizes its proper place in service to something greater.

Fulfillment implies not confusing the roles, identities, personae, and characters one performs in life with one's true north. Only the central core of being offers the radiance of aliveness true to self. Its vitality whispers, connecting the known with the unknown, experientially unifying the individual with the origin of the force of creativity.

Searching for bestowed mission when the aspects of being are fragmented is like looking for an object in the dark. Feeling more comprehensively allows perceiving things more coherently. Identity that opens itself to the appropriate quality for a given situation or rush of energy does not make the same anxiety-driven decisions.

As attention unifies with experience, it turns up the light, illuminating self's previously unseen exalted pathway. Osensei's process changed his identity not toward something new, but rather toward something more original. When he described himself as the universe, he transcended the limits of what seemed possible, offering a path for humanity to explore. Once we peer into a night sky less obscured by ambient light, the previously invisible appears.

PART TWO

AIKIDO:
OSENSEI'S PROCESS

Aikido in Three Easy Lessons

FEEL WHERE YOU ARE
Feel where you are tight.
Feel where you are relaxed.
Feel where you are in your life.
Feel where you are in Creation.
Presence / Rhythm

       HARMONIOUS RELATIONSHIP
       The essence of Aikido cultivates reconciliation.
       Align with the situation as it unfolds.
       Move in concert.
       Adaptability / Harmony

SHARE WHO YOU ARE
Express your energy. Lead.
Make your contribution.
Let yourself be seen.
Creativity / Melody

5

LOVE THE MYSTERY

HISTORICAL ORIGINS

Aikido's roots date back through the martial form of Daito-ryu Aiki-jujitsu all the way back to the Yagyu School of Sword originating in Japan around the fifteenth century. Although its origins can be traced back to ancient Japanese martial tradition, Aikido is a modern art founded in the mid-twentieth century.

Morihei Ueshiba, the founder of Aikido, is referred to as Osensei. Sensei, in Japanese, means "teacher" and implies "one who has gone before," one who helps others find their path. Osensei means "great teacher," or "teacher of teachers." Born in 1883, Osensei died in 1969.

In one story, due to an early experience of seeing his father beaten by a group of thugs, Morihei Ueshiba became increasingly interested in strength and developing martial skills. In another, he trained at an intense level of devotion to overcome an illness in earlier life. Regardless of what sent him down his path, the stories of his devotion to the study and the intensity of his practice are legendary. He studied many arts and became a master of sword and spear. Osensei was an instructor in the School of Daitu-ryu Aiki-jujitsu (which purportedly informed the training of America's Secret Service agents) as well as several other forms of open-handed combat.

Although he was never defeated in combat, he was not satisfied with martial strength. He spent many years searching for a deeper meaning to the training. He took numerous journeys in search of greater wisdom and spiritual transcendence. At one point in his life, he had an enlightenment experience, an important moment in the birth of the unique path of Aikido:

> Suddenly the earth trembled. Golden vapor welled up from the ground and engulfed me. I felt transformed into a golden image, and my body seemed as light as a feather. All at once I understood the nature of creation: the Way of a Warrior is to manifest Divine Love, a spirit that embraces and nurtures all things. Tears of gratitude and joy streamed down my cheeks. I saw the entire earth as my home, and the sun, moon, and stars as my intimate friends. All attachment to material things vanished . . . (Morihei Ueshiba, *The Art of Peace*, trans. and ed. John Stevens, Boston: Shambhala, 2002, 11)

The word *Aikido* is made up of three kanji—pictographs or syllables—describing several important concepts that make Aikido unique and applicable. *Ai* means both "love" and "harmony," and signifies confluence, coming together, and unity. *Ki* originally means "steam," implying universal energy, vital force, mind, spirit, mood, adaptability, and common sense. *Do* means a way of knowledge, art, or life path.

The concept of Ki implies that Aikido takes place in the domain of energy, the hidden realm, which activates and manifests the physical realm. And the kanji *Do* describes a path implying ongoing growth and development. *Aikido* can be translated as "the Way of Harmony with the spirit of the Universe." It is the Path (Do) of Love and Harmony (Ai), with the Divine Spirit of Infinite Creativity, the energy of creation (Ki).

> "As the symbol Ai - harmony is common with the symbol Ai - love, I decided to name my unique budo Aikido . . . It is a great love omnipresent in all quarters and all times of the universe. There is

no enemy of love. There is no discord in love. Aikido is the realization of love." (Morihei Ueshiba, Osensei, quoted in Kisshomaru Ueshiba, *Aikido*, trans. Kazuaki Tanahashi and Roy Maurer, Tokyo: Hozansha; San Francisco: Japan Publications, 1974)

Aikido grew out of the warrior arts of the east. The Japanese term for the warrior's domain is *budo*. The word budo is made up of two kanji. *Do* means a path, a way of life, a life inquiry into a way of being; *bu*, the symbol for warrior, signifies the idea of stopping or ending war, implying the ability to create peace. War is inimical to the growth and development of an individual or a society.

Budo, commonly translated as "the Way of the Warrior," implies the protection of society's growth and development. Budo, ancient samurai tradition, was a culture of service to a larger good. In the modern world, it translates as the way of leadership, the path of one who takes responsibility for more than oneself—for society and the world at large.

In the realm of the spirit, the possibility of stopping the war (within) pivots on resolving inner conflicts. Aikido, through blending with the Ki, the energy or force of an attacker in the manifest realm, aligns us in a harmonious relationship with Ki, the force of creation, thus experientially becoming the bridge that unifies the realms. On a personal level, it starts with harmonizing attention, the focus of awareness, experiencing the vitality flowing into and through aliveness. It extends to one's action in the world and completes the universe through an ongoing and continual alignment of a harmonious relationship with the mystery.

AWARENESS POSITION AND POWER

The domain of the martial arts refers to studies in the realm of Mars, the god of war. Distinct from the world of sport, where there are rules, the art of war exists in a realm where there are none. There are no boundaries to the universe of war, and as a life-and-death matter, war is spooky beyond belief. In the martial metaphor, effectiveness decides life and death. On the edge of survival, to be effective means maximum result with minimal expenditure of energy. Laser focus of energy, positioning force to the greatest effect, is paramount.

Martial arts in the physical realm focus primarily on external position to control or vanquish an attacking opponent. The outer, visible, or technical aspects of training each apply to a specific situation. Meanwhile, at the same time, the finer dimensions of inner experiential alignment apply in all times and quarters of the universe. Aikido is commonly recognized and understood as the application of physical movements that neutralize an attack, but this describes only the external, the "martial" application of the art. The founder repeatedly emphasized that in its deeper sense, Aikido harmonizes humanity's relationship individually and collectively with the creative force of the universe. Beyond creating stronger individuals, it creates a stronger society leading to a beautiful world.

Translated to the realms of business, science, education, and relationship, the principle of harmony still rules. Effective action works in harmony with the laws of the universe. Applying energy to open a door in the direction it swings can be described as intelligent, fitting, and in harmony with the way it swings. Harmony is intelligent and intelligence is harmonious. The way of Aiki defines a more intelligent, useful, and beautifully enriching path than forcing, opposing, or resisting. Harmony implies functioning intelligently, in the most effective way, toward a desired result. In daily life, harmonious engagement implies engendering intelligent action in the world.

In a life-threatening situation, precision focus is the essence of the moment. A rush of energy, a force within, kinesthetically activates, superseding any internal conversation. A holistic somatic network—a field of energy in a finer dimension—claims command of action. This happens to the tiniest degree in the continual autonomic correction of each minuscule loss of balance and proprioceptive reaction.

The action of Aikido lives in the divine realm of the origin of creation as it manifests the hidden world of energy and the observable world of matter. In Aikido, power implies blending with the intention, sourcing the neural signals that activate the movement of the muscles driving the kinesthetic action—the physical movement of the attacker. The whole sequence producing movement is an aftereffect of intent, or Ki. As such, if the position and timing of action are harmonious, a small movement at the original source produces a disproportionate effect in the corresponding action and ultimate outcome.

The rush of Ki, the spirit's call to action, is often identified as fear when we are in a state of overwhelm—a story that, once repeated, leads to a destiny. When we practice a story of Aiki, that same energy fuels the journey into one's best operating place and a fulfilling life. Common to any master or champion is an ongoing process of exploring how to position the location of attention in one's best operating place.

UNIFYING MARTIAL STUDY AND SPIRITUAL PRACTICE

Any advanced martial artist works on quality of being as a fundamental basis for technical skill, as well as to create more coherence in life. The hours applied to the study of the external form of the arts, and especially to the seemingly subtle internal aspects, relative to the amount of time the skills are applied in ordinary life, may make the study appear a questionable investment. Return on investment, should those abilities ever be needed, changes that equation. Both the prospect of a violent attacker and the prospect of an unfulfilling life raise the stakes exponentially.

When we resist the pressure of the energy of change, it feels like a problem. That is one story. In another story, through flowing with change, the energies, pressure, or impetus offer guidance, new ideas, and creative possibilities. As we yield location and move into a position of influence, yin becomes yang, and receptivity becomes creativity. Becoming one with the energy that initiates the attack, when done strategically, establishes harmonious relationship and empowers the ability to lead change. Power is free energy, disposable income. When proper alignment exists between circle and center, power transports one from a state of victimhood at the mercy of energy labeled as fear, into responsibility, a choice of warrior spirit. The spiritual journey to a sense of experiential presence generates a field of creative options and possibilities and frees destiny from the limited reactive behavior of the basal ganglia, *and* any potential negative influence from the default mode network. Presence determines worth, impact, and power of contribution.

Hearing means allowing information into conscious awareness. Listening in Aiki lets us complete the steps of receiving, evaluating, and acting on the information. A spirit of loving harmony listens, following the exalted guidance of the whisperings. Down the path of Aiki, listening journeys to peaceful reconciliation, a life of loving protection. Love gives birth to harmony, and this birthing is the power that transforms the reptilian-based reactive discord of entrenched opposition into the joy that comes from a spirit of listening and exploring understanding.

The messages found in subtle feeling, through the somatic system, are whisperings of the exalted workings, offering guidance in negotiating the change unfolding. In a spirit of listening, one can hear the purpose behind the force expressing an attack or causing change. When harmonious intent deals with energy at its original source, peaceful reconciliation becomes not only possible but almost inevitable.

DO AND WAZA:
PRINCIPLES AND TECHNIQUES

Aikido represents a path, the way of Aiki, living the spiritual *principles* of improvisational harmony with the source of creation. The term *Aiki-waza* describes the *techniques* generated out of those principles, used to handle a situation in the physical realm.

The term *Do* (pronounced "doe" with a long "o"), the third syllable in Aikido, indicates a path, a way, principles creating a philosophy. The way or path of Aiki describes a life experience of aligning with the forces that give birth to creativity and the creation. Aikido aligns with creating life out of the principles that inform the art.

Waza means "techniques," and in the martial realm it implies the visible movements, commonly confused for or understood by a beginner or the uninitiated to be the art itself. The term Aiki-waza describes the techniques developed out of Aiki principles, used to neutralize an attack in the physical realm. The meaning expands and can be applied beyond the martial realm, to precision-effective technical function in the material world across disciplines.

Training differentiates two aspects: study of the principles, or *benkyo*; and *keiko*, the practice of techniques. The word keiko is comprised of two characters that mean "to think" and "the past," and together they mean to train and study the teaching of the past. The Do, the way or path of Aiki, opens into the future.

The dictionary defines technique as the mechanical or formal part of an art. Techniques teach the method and procedure of the execution of an art or craft. Principles describe universal laws and fundamental truths that govern action, the ultimate basis on which something depends—the cause, in the widest sense. Techniques apply specifically to a given situation. Principles apply universally. Martial techniques in the physical domain are the strikes, pins, wristlocks, and projection throws utilized to physically handle an attacker. Principles in the physical domain might be fluidity, balance, and alignment of position.

Principles help distill usable understanding of a universe that is too vast and complex to comprehend. The enhanced perception that principles distill amplifies ability to interact creatively with the whole of life. When options surface, this increases the likelihood of attaining desirable outcomes. The divine spirit of Aikido designed the art to serve the completion of each individual. The reconciliation of Aikido unifies the field of being and creates solutions in harmony with the essence of a situation or an entity's unique nature.

Resonance goes back and forth between techniques as subatomic particles, and simultaneously flows as unformed potential—and in this way, training forges transformational technique that emerges from another dimension in the same time-space. Training traces the waza back, returning to the source that produces techniques and forms. The path leads to the mystery, that which creates the principles and movements, the origin, the divine realms.

Osensei used the term Aikido both when he referred to the mat practice of the waza—the physical techniques—as well as to the larger alchemical study of the workings of universal harmony. He taught the techniques, the physical practice of Aiki, as the pathway to train and develop the Do, the way of harmoniously responding to a changing universe. The kaleidoscopic appearance of forms in the manifest world emanates out when we embody the principles. The power of Aiki is demonstrated in the physical realm. Its possibility radiates through the whole of creation.

His interest went beyond teaching a martial art. It was his intention to convey a process. He did so through a martial arts form because that was his lineage. Osensei taught the principles to kabuki dancers and baseball players. The writings he left predominantly explore the creative aspect of the art. He wrote almost nothing about technical form. Osensei was teaching the way of harmony to reconcile the individual and the whole of the manifest world with the mystery.

He offered it hoping the world would extend the magic that he showed in the martial arts to all the realms of art, science, commerce, education, and spiritual development. Nadeau Sensei emphasized that Osensei was very explicit about his priority in teaching, expressing a fervent hope that people would take the process beyond the dojo and apply the way of harmony throughout all domains of human ability.

Osensei explained that he taught through the martial art metaphor because that was his path. His intention in sharing the art was for each person to apply the process in their art or profession. He wanted each person to excel in what they did, for each person to come to fulfillment, to completion, to excel in expressing their exalted workings at an extraordinary level.

Through the window of the larger study of universal harmony, physical forms as coded messages reveal a path to the fundamental principles about how the universe works. Deepening the understanding of principles empowers the ability to create, adapt, and expand beyond the known, beyond existing techniques that one has learned. That is what the founder did. Though he presented his wisdom through a martial arts frame, he was interested in teaching and inspiring people to embrace a process, because every step of realigning into the central core of the unified field experience transforms the unfolding.

Through the principles of Aiki, Aikido creatively produces Aiki-waza in the dojo and beyond. The principles of inner alignment similarly produce a harmonious effectiveness in the office or shop, on the field, or with the children. Whether in an individual, a family, a business, an educational system, or a society, the fundamentals apply. In every domain, techniques appear spontaneously as if by magic. It isn't really magic—or rather, it is and it isn't. It is the power of harmony, Aikido, the unified field.

The many paths up Mount Fuji fundamentally arrive at a common outcome. Connected to the universe through the central core, the essential doorway of self, each person's path to the summit will follow its own course. Aikido, enjoying the unified field experience, leads an individual on the exalted path, fitting with and leading them to the completion of their unique makeup or nature.

OSENSEI'S PROCESS: AIKIDO

Physically, Aikido emphasizes the principle of harmony through the action and technique of moving "off the line" of an attack. Blending into harmonious relationship with energy changes the energy. Whether the challenge faced is an attack or the force of change, positioning oneself in harmonious relationship with Ki, both internally and externally, transforms experience. Rather than receiving or blocking, harmonious relationship redirects threatening energy, making it available to be led. Returning to source translates in human relationship as understanding the needs driving a person's intentions, which appear in the manifest world as their words and actions.

Blending transforms energy, allowing it to be utilized as a basis for the quality and power of any technique that may be applied in and beyond the martial realms. The external form and exercises are visible, tangible practices that develop, aligning internal positioning in harmony with the force of aliveness. Once the principles are internalized as the essence of the art, the way of harmony becomes the basis for one's quality of life.

It was the founder's recognition of internal positioning into the dimensional shift and the extraordinary state of power produced that catapulted Aikido into its unique position in the world. The creation of Aikido came about through Osensei listening to the whisperings of the Aiki Kami, the divine spirit of Aikido.

As the story goes, the Aiki Kami would wake him up in the middle of the night, take him out in the garden, and teach him to unify yin and yang in a spirit of harmony. The Kami taught the energetic process through Osensei's lineage: the martial arts, the technical forms of Aiki-jujitsu.

The concept of positioning in one's best operating place is a fundamental practice for any martial artist or champion athlete, or for anyone who reaches or even approaches a level of mastery. Osensei, by positioning himself in an internal realm of finer energies that approached the origin of the creative force, experienced a dimensional shift that produced an enlightenment experience, from which grew a quantum leap in function. After the earlier described experience in which "golden vapor welled up from the ground" and engulfed him, his art did more than just change—it made a quantum leap, a dimensional shift.

Osensei's study with the Kami opened the path, transforming the earlier techniques into the modern forms identified commonly as Aikido. The older form of Aiki-jujitsu taught techniques formed out of non-resistance to the energy of an attacker's force. Osensei was seeing another potential step beyond simply not opposing an attacker's force, beyond going with it or using it against them. He said the previous arts he had studied had been discerned by the human mind. Aiki taught by the Kami was formless, emanating from the divine creative force.

He repeatedly emphasized manifesting technique out of an all-encompassing single source or unified field. The unification of the essence of being with the source and totality of the universe in the divine realm of the Kami is the original practice of Ai. Religious arts describe it as loving God. Through the power of love, Osensei shifted into a dimension that included and potentially transformed the energy of an attacker, resolving the conflict and in the degree of the moment, creating a beautiful world.

His process, unifying the polarities with the field, took best operating place through a quantum leap into ever-finer and increasingly inexplicable dimensions, toward the origin of creativity. Drawing on ancient Japanese mythology, he described the above process as standing on the floating bridge of heaven. Reportedly, Osensei spoke ceaselessly of the floating bridge of heaven and its importance in the creation of Aiki, saying, "You must stand on the floating bridge of heaven. If you do not stand on the floating bridge of heaven, Aiki will not come forth."

The Shinto myth of "standing on the floating bridge of heaven" comes from the *Kojiki* (*Records of Ancient Matters*), an ancient Japanese sacred text and creation myth. In this myth, a bridge connects heaven and earth. Standing on this bridge, the dual forces of the universe —creative and receptive, represented by the gods Izanagi and Izanami, the masculine and feminine principles of creation—dipped a sword into the ocean. As they withdrew it, drops dripping off the sword created the islands of Japan. Through the power of myth, the story of the bridge describes the mystical force of unification that combines the polarity of creation, fashioning everything from a single first magnetic vibration into the ever-changing present structure or form of the universal mass.

Standing on the floating bridge of heaven, it becomes clear that the two locations and the bridge that connects them symbolize embodying the continuum of the trinity of creativity—that is, the mysterious creating force, the creation being manifest, and the unified field encompassing the polarities. The three interdependent aspects combine: the two poles and the magnetic field, definable elements yet inseparable in their existence. Standing on the floating bridge of heaven expands superposition and quantum entanglement experientially, unifying the manifest and divine realms. To stand on the floating bridge is to manifest heavenly energies in the earthly realm until $1 + 1 = 1$, on earth as it is in heaven.

The bridge is a metaphor for the magic of unification. It describes the process of the force that attracts, combines, and unifies seemingly disparate energies, opposing forces, or aspects in any field. Hydrogen and oxygen unify to become water. In Aiki-land, the interpenetrating forces—upward rising and downward sinking, form and flow, composition and improvisation, mind and body, thoughts and feelings, breathing in and breathing out, talking and listening, day and night, the divine and the manifest realms, and all dynamic polarities in the unified field—harmonize with and complete each other. These seeming polarities simultaneously create and are created out of the whole system interdependently.

In the process of Aikido, standing on the floating bridge implies standing in both realms, one creating one being created, one foot metaphorically in each at the same time. It defines experiencing self as the field that includes and unifies both. Standing on the floating bridge of heaven expresses connecting to the origins of Ki while standing and functioning in the manifest realm.

Osensei taught a process of shifting into a superlative dimension of best operating place, achieving effective function at a level that transformed his domain of martial arts, comparable to how the study of quantum theory transformed physics. The mystical quantum connection between unformed potential and subatomic particles crossed the bridge. Around that same era, coincidentally, the story of jazz expressed something of a quantum leap in music, demonstrating the unity between the world of form and the void.

At that time, Aikido was taught in the tradition of the martial arts. For many, martial skills were the purpose of their training. It was what brought them through the door. The finer dimensions Osensei was positioning himself in were not perceived nor even sought by many. He was dealing in finer dimensions, which inevitably look mystical to an awareness that is focused in the manifest realm. He spoke a unique dialect. He spoke in the abstract. He drew on imagery from Shinto mythology.

The mysticism of his language confused many who, as a result, primarily focused their practice on the physical aspect of the technical forms. Without the clarity that what one is truly refining is one's ability to operate as original source, the practice looks like repeating forms. In any case, the physical was visible, accessible, easy to apprehend. It was also the understanding of some—those who held a deeper level of interest—that repeating these techniques was the doorway to accessing the finer dimensions.

In the potential field of the ocean of energy, the understanding and focus of attention in the finer realms is the central focal point. Aikido is, as its name implies, a process of feeling the oneness of the creator, the creative process, and the creation—all at the same time. It is unification, both *into and with* the original experiential field out of which everything emanates.

The art of the warrior stops war and creates peace. The concept of budo, so often misconstrued as being about fighting, causes some to default to channeling energy into the tools, practices, and science of destruction. The art of peace focuses on the creation of beauty in the relationship of individuals and the universal. The art of the Kami intentionally positions the mindset of creativity in a spirit of love. The fulfillment of the individual through unification with the universal has the potential to produce a field of resonance by which the world is miraculously charmed, leading people to live harmoniously together in peace.

The physical practice in an Aikido dojo offers an excellent feedback mechanism. The practice improves one's alignment in the physical dimension, as does any physical discipline to some degree. Yet this improvement need not start or stop there. The founder said, "Heaven is where one is standing, and that is the place to train."

Through the teachings of the divine spirit of Aikido, Osensei developed and shared a process of continually repositioning the location of attention in a spirit of harmony. The power of harmony aligns attention into dimensions on the threshold of the mystery where, as in quantum mechanics, possibility transcends the laws of classical physics. Intentionally positioning attention in harmonious relationship to Ki, standing on the floating bridge of heaven, forms the fundamental teaching.

He was better on some days than others. When his attention to the experiential process diminished, all the knowledge he possessed of the art didn't work as well, even for him. Osensei, too, had to perform the process repeatedly in each moment. At times, he would stop teaching or demonstrating and step to the side, pause for a moment, and do his process, whether chanting or some physical action, or a spiraling move he repeatedly did with the staff. He had various approaches to making the dimensional shift.

A main recurrent theme of his process was embodying Ichi Rei, Shi Kon, San Gen, and Hachi Riki—the unification of the four spirits, the three realms, and the eight powers, within the one source or one light. Nadeau Sensei described the forms of process Osensei used to shift dimensionally, returning to the one source, as "travel vehicles." Using one of his travel vehicles, such as chanting, centering, or practices and rituals to connect with the universe, he would reposition attention and stand on the floating bridge of heaven that unified the field.

Then, coming back into action in the manifest realm, he would step onto the mat and he would be different. When he activated his process of making a dimensional shift, his technique became more powerful and less visible. Sometimes he would pause and shift a second or third time. His techniques appeared to be magic, and his abilities defied explanation. He could throw without touching, affect people from a distance, and effortlessly demonstrate inconceivable ability. He changed himself, and by doing so, he also changed the curvature of time-space so that it was no longer limited by what should have been possible or impossible.

When asked why the students could not reproduce what he did, the founder said he understood the harmony of yin and yang as a natural law at a level the students did not. His universal harmony reached such an encompassing level that he could transform the yang energy of attack into a yin force that received the influence of his technique effortlessly, even joyfully.

His mission was teaching his students how to make a dimensional shift from ordinary consciousness into one's best operating place, to develop and realize potential that exceeds what imagination envisions. Emphasizing the Do, the way of being of harmonious relationship, potentially refines and inculcates the principle that the universe, the lives of each individual, and the culture of society interpenetrate as one system.

Even in Osensei's later years, when he often had difficulty walking up the stairs, he could still step onto the mat and, through his process, transform himself and gracefully handle multiple attackers. He described himself differently in the two distinct locations, with the terms "this old man" and "Ueshiba of Aikido." Describing Osensei's change as a "dimensional shift," Nadeau Sensei emphasized that "it wasn't the same person."

BEST OPERATING PLACE

Normally a person turns up the rheostat of attention when their interest rises, or based on whether the situation in question is critical. Beyond technique, the process of moving attention from casual, to paying attention, to a life-and-death-critical level of focus, and finally into one's best operating place, is an underlying central principle of mastery in any art. When the center of attention operates in conjunction with the center of aliveness through the physical being, the field of potential enlivens.

When the light of attention shines on it, best operating place becomes an exploration. Because best operating place is not a fixed point. It is an experience of the moment, vital and moving like everything in the universe, just as energy is itself movement, change, transformation. Conscious of the possibility, attention can create systems and patterns that enable living an increasing percentage of life moving toward rather than away from best operating place. Aikido experientially develops the positive power of story, synaptic connections, and systems of thought to establish ever-finer levels of best operating place. Each realignment of position serves as the base for the next step in a constant process of growth and development.

From beginner to champion, virtually everyone has some kind of process or ritual as they prepare for the performance of action that matters to them. A golfer about to take a shot never just walks up and hits the ball. To get ready, they always stand there for a moment and, whether they think about it or not, execute a little process to position attention into their best operating place. The external aspects are visible, the internal hidden. It is a process that coordinates mind, body, and spirit into a unified field until they "feel just right." Everyone uses some form of process before they do anything that matters to them.

Typically, in some varying order, golfers wiggle the club a few times, then step up to the ball, getting ready and practicing the shot in their imagination. Then they feel the club again and usually step back and practice the shot a couple times, swinging away from the ball. Next, they step back up to the ball, shifting their weight back and forth before they approach shooting position. When they're done with this process to the degree that they require to prepare for the seriousness of the challenge, they hit the ball. Everyone who plays the game will do some form of this process on every shot.

A baseball player, in that moment between the time they come out of the dugout and the time they step into the batter's box, engages in their version of an intentionally practiced process, which they repeat again as they prepare for each pitch. A basketball player who is about to take a free throw will never just walk up and take the shot—never. They always have a little process of adjustments, bouncing the ball until they "feel just right."

Feeling is a reboot. Feeling is now. Feeling processes energy, turning the rush of potential disturbance into usable power. Energy and attention unify in the realm of feeling. They are an interactive wave-particle quantum entanglement. They give birth to each other.

Lawyers preparing for the summation, executives going into an important meeting, salespeople on the edge of a big deal, and performers just about to go on stage, all shift through a process. It may be elaborate. It may be as simple as a single breath. Given a conscious moment before entering any critical performance or challenge, though they may not be aware of it, almost everybody does "the breath thing."

Similar to a musician tuning their instrument until it feels right on, anyone who excels in their field trains to feel when the attention locates in the center of the energy and everything "feels just right." Whatever the approach, a process is initiated, often just below the threshold of consciousness but near enough to be sensed. It is a movement of the location of attention, enabling energy to activate technique more coherently. Training takes the positioning process from needing a moment, to a second, to a fraction of a second, to a nanosecond.

Usually the more an action or performance matters, the more the practitioner goes back and forth between the "form practice" of lining up and preparing for action, and the "internal process" of getting into their best operating place until they feel right. The process starts with feeling center, the internal shift in the location of attention, and moves to aligning center-circle, the subtle force, in relationship to action in the outer world. The process is an experiential dialogue between mind and body that aligns the two as a unity, $1 + 1 = 1$, a unified field of being.

Athletes might speak of "the inner game" when they refer to getting into a place internally that feels just right. Martial studies also refer to internal and external arts, applying the same basic distinction. Commonly, on the threshold of performance, everyone from beginners to masters has a "process" to get into their best operating place or at least move toward it. Some people rub a rabbit's foot or semi-consciously effect some neural-linguistic trigger that "feels better."

Most everyone has utilized some physical process that equates to centering, connecting to ground, and opening the channels that allow the energy to flow, without ever having heard this sequence of words. For some it happens below the conscious level. For others it is the essence of conscious training. When a master in their field sets up to prepare the external aspects of a move, such as the distances required, the master is also setting up internally, aligning the flow of energy and moving it from its source to the objective of its delivery, thus consciously and intentionally completing the universe.

MASTERY

A master spends their life studying and developing high-speed precision access to a location of power through the focus of intent, developing the power of intent in the process, Aikido takes both best operating place and the power of intent through the warp of a dimensional shift. Aiki initiates a quantum leap to an extraordinary level of love, harmony, and joy. The inevitable outcome—extraordinary, innovative effectiveness—is, as the founder described it, the dust after the technique.

In the martial realm, it is less that a master knows exactly what to do. Rather, they know what to do when they don't know what to do. Peak performance in martial arts is usually required for a relatively brief engagement, however intensely focused. In superposition, mastery forges exceptional practice while releasing it into the unknown moment of becoming. During the entry into execution, mastery enables the endless hours of precision preparation to dissolve into allowing the mystery. Unifying both the practice and the mystery at the same time, in the same time-space of $1 + 1 = 1$, opens infinite possibility, manifesting infinite creativity.

Aikido training develops speed of response, correcting the discomfort that we feel from the shock of the rush when we are unprepared. Once activated, the magnetism of the central core attracts and harmonizes the aspects of being into alignment. The unified field of being, emanating out of its original state, expresses its fullness without reservation while maintaining harmony with the universe the whole time. The primary directive of the training is the focus of attention into exploration of best operating place, which translates reactivity into a call to action, producing seemingly inexplicable functional power.

Bu, the Japanese symbol for the warrior's domain, primarily implies training a warrior's spirit. Before a warrior can be effective in action, that warrior's first challenge is to galvanize a unified field of function—after which they can direct and attempt to implement action. From there, water naturally flows downhill. The shift into finer levels of awareness and experience is the ticket to a quantum leap in level of consciousness, perception, function, and ultimately quality of life. The inner process, precision alignment between intention and activation, opens a dimensional doorway to exponential power. This process refines itself forever in anyone interested enough to follow the journey into mastery, which, rather than a fixed destination, implies ongoing growth and development.

UNEXPECTED ATTACK SITUATIONS

A fight is often something of an agreement, certainly in a case where one person could walk away. An encounter in that realm could almost be classified under the category of sport. Martial arts prepare the practitioner for war, a very different scenario. Training prepares one for the most challenging martial situations, those involving unexpected attack. Being surprised, unprepared, or facing unexpected violence from an attack that comes out of nowhere with no option of escape, presents the greatest challenge.

Attackers favor surprise attack because the first action can be so decisive. Evading the target's attention is the basis of a surprise attack. It gives the advantage of having one's forces assembled while the opponent is unable to take action and is still trying to cohere, assess, and strategize. When the target's attention is focused elsewhere, the degree of an attack's effectiveness is in direct proportion to the time it takes to cross the gap between the center of attention and the glow of Ki. The battle can be over before the opposing army can assemble their forces or unify their field.

To prevent this possibility, a fighting force can develop a rapid-response unit trained to expect a surprise attack. This training would develop the fighters' ability to go from the awareness of an alert to functioning readiness in the shortest time possible. Success depends on the time it takes to become present, because that is the critical function. Only then is it possible to tune attention to perceive the situation, process the data, and know what to do with any change or challenge.

In the face of surprise, the capacity to handle the rush of energy and assemble a coherent, unified alive system of action determines the degree of effectiveness in function as much as, if not more than, technical skill training. Training commonly focuses on the technical aspect of the art, developing it into automatic muscle memory because the element of speed is so important. Even though the move may have been trained sufficiently and fire off instantaneously, it doesn't do so until attention completes the preliminary steps and issues the signal.

In the face of the unexpected, one must first develop a strategy as quickly as possible in order to have the power to execute it before it is too late. Getting in the driver's seat, starting the engine, and shifting into drive before stepping on the gas and turning the wheel, is a metaphor for first locating attention in the center of power and activating all the systems needed. The internal process takes place in the hidden realm but relies on the same concept. Aiki mastery exploration develops access to an exceptional dimension of capability, at a speed unseen by the human eye.

The transition period from being surprised, to recognizing the situation, to aligning to it in the proper stance and adjusting position, appropriately transforms yang and yin, making all the difference in the world. The call to battle stations is the journey from letting attention be distracted elsewhere, to focusing attention into feeling, and operating with attention in the driver's seat, the center of the intensity of the rush. The precision of the dimensional shift defines the potential functional power of response.

The rush of energy and corresponding startle complex stimulate the evolutionarily developed reactivity of withdrawal to happen unconsciously. Recognizing the potential startle effect of the rush allows and reinforces the intentional shift of synaptic pathways into best operating place for each unique moment of each unique situation. Through practice, one potentially develops Aiki as the primary response preceding any action. Adapting position continuously into a harmonious relationship with a changing universe achieves an extraordinary best operating place. Action appropriate to the constant flow of change naturally flows out of returning feeling to source.

Harmonizing with the energy of surprise—whether the endless small rushes of daily life or a huge rush like an urgent, life-changing decision or a life-threatening attack—is a process that must be done in an orderly fashion, like building a house. First the foundation is established. Then the frame goes on top of the foundation, and then the siding goes on the frame. Osensei talked about the importance of Aikido being performed in an orderly fashion: one, two, three.

Step one is standing on the floating bridge of heaven for Aiki to come forth. Proper training inculcates focus on positioning location internally, "coming from a good place," before applying a technique or initiating any action. In step two, the positioning of the physical structure comes forth from a centered, grounded, flowing state. For step three, one is present and centered. Located in the most effective position, one then applies the technique, delivers the strike, or performs the action; one builds the house or sings the song. Orderly.

As a house built on a weak foundation may be fine until a storm, so may ordinary consciousness, until, in the face of the potential energetic fragmentation of surprise, its functioning falls to pieces. Osensei demonstrated the infinite potential embedded in the mystery of the precision spiritual journey, from being "out of it" to being centered, and from being "centered enough to feel OK" to being transformationally united with the center of the universe.

The fundamental challenge a warrior faces, and the foundation on which the effectiveness of martial skill rests, is calming the spirit and returning wholly and totally to a coherent energy focus, empowering operation from a solid base. The physical practice absorbs the kinetic energy of a physical attack, using it for the application of technique. The same principle applies internally to utilizing the intensity of the rush, absorbing it by blending with it. Through the power of harmony, Ki enhances both joy and function in the application of a creative response to any challenge or job.

6

BREATHE THE HARMONY

AI KI DO in one easy Lesson
Continually Realign Harmonious Participation

CENTER CIRCLE

The functioning level of the alive system depends on center-circle relationship as being fundamental in empowering technical application and life fulfillment. Generating spontaneous, infinite, improvisational creativity, harmony empowers technical processes, in the martial realms and beyond. Spiritual surplus, infinite creative possibility, emanates generosity that is projected into the world. It opens possibility. Focusing into presence, centering, bringing attention into experience, and inhaling the power of harmony, all radiate a glow of attraction curving time-space—in other words, changing reality.

Peak performance lexicon references best operating place with terms like being *balanced, centered, grounded, in the zone,* or *in flow state.* In executive performance, the words might change to describe having confidence, exhibiting leadership, or "generating" a positive spirit. In the arts or in sports, people to tell each other to get "it together" or get "with it." A musical performance might be "really with it" or "right on." All the terminology points to a location where the dual aspects of being inner and outer align, where mind and body unify $1 + 1 = 1$ into an exponential transformation, a dimensional shift, a quantum leap in strategic design as well as functional capability.

Whatever the challenge, superlative function emanates from positioning attention in best operating place. With practice the process develops synaptic pathways, making dimensional transformation of capability the basis of entry into every engagement. Training allows us to develop consciously, and to reposition while functioning in action; both happen at the same time.

Waking up fully present and being able to handle every situation, every turn in the conversation, every unexpected change in life circumstances, may be a dream goal. Winston Churchill defines success as going from failure to failure with no loss of enthusiasm. Osensei called failure the key to success, saying that each mistake teaches something. A goal is a story, one that has little use if it isn't a dream we cherish. Its value comes from its usefulness, not its veracity.

The journey into best operating place is potentially life-and-death critical in the face of a surprise attack. Less critical yet still valuable, the power of harmony applies in every situation, with every pulse and wave of universal energy. Continually adjusting position toward the unified field experience—with self, with one's training partners, with life, in all times and all quarters of the universe—is Aiki.

THE CENTER OF THE CENTER

Each movement on approach to center is smaller in distance and subtler in experience. As they get smaller, they seem relatively inconsequential. Re-centering with each seemingly endless rush of energy all day long seems less important than the tasks of life that seem so pressing. Getting a little more centered, while important, is overshadowed and undervalued, then postponed. Each small rush is an individual fragment, but when combined, they assemble into life's destiny. Even alignment a fraction of a degree off, if not corrected, causes failure to arrive at the intended port. Especially in strong winds, a sailor is continually attentive to the sails, tiller, and wind, realigning the balance that each finer adjustment holds. In Aiki-land, that translates to center, ground, and flow.

Each finer move, in aligning with center, requires even greater attention to be perceived. And because these moves require more attention yet seem smaller and of less importance, their value is easily underestimated, undervalued, and abandoned. Counterintuitively, each smaller increment on approach to central core has increasingly dramatic effects on the spirit's journey.

Through practice the system learns that as the adjustments get finer, they have greater effect on the transformation of being and the quality of life. As the difference between a gold and silver medal can be one hundredth of a second, mastery seeks precision, which might seem inconsequential to the average person. In the entry into the unknown dimensions of the central core, the value of center increases exponentially with each finer step.

SIGNS AND SIGNALS

When someone is highly effective, they are said to be "with it" or "on it." When we are feeling off-center, we use terms like "out of it," "out of sorts," "off," or just "having a bad day." "Out of it" accurately describes attention out of connection with the central core of Ki, the vitality of life. When feeling "out of it," one easily misses the bus or drifts into another lane. Without a spiritual practice, our state, attitude, or mood just *happens*. Whenever center and circle go out of balance, it is easy to "lose it." The good news is that with a simple understanding of the process, it is easy to correct. As Nadeau Sensei points out, "When you're out of it . . . it is still there."

Because although there are times and places in life where it is easy to get lost, there are guiding signs and warning signals to lead one home. Though, unless we are looking for them and also trained to read them, the guidance can too often be missed. The oil light on the dashboard goes on when a car's engine needs oil—not a big issue, unless ignored.

"Losing it," falling asleep, as well as over-excitement or distraction can cause one to miss the signals. In the middle of an intense situation, the rush of energy can overwhelm. Attention and experience disconnect. Awareness virtually blacks out, and in extreme cases it literally does. When consciousness loses connection with feeling, it loses the ability to hear or read the signals and subsequently fails to correct.

When we are not paying attention or are so excited that our attention loses focus, we don't realize that no one is driving. Once "out of it," awareness does not feel, cannot, so there's no awareness present to make corrections. Before the process of correction can begin to activate, someone who knows that the corrections need to be made must get in the driver's seat. Because once awareness senses clarity of need and locates appropriately, the corrections are negotiable, both simple and easy.

The little bumps in between lanes on the freeway are signals that warn a driver if they are drifting out of their lane. When receiving the signals, a driver simply positions back into the correct location before an accident occurs. One can set an alarm clock to signal when the bus is coming. Whether adding oil, setting an alarm, or simply turning the steering wheel or handlebars ever so slightly, adjusting course is not that big of a deal.

On the highway of life, it is not shifting back into the center of the lane that is hard. The problem is falling asleep at the wheel or succumbing to distractions, positioning attention on the wrong focus. When we fail to appreciate and utilize the warning signals, or sleep through the alarm, the bus is missed, or the journey ends in a wrong destination or an accident. The challenge is prioritizing life strategy appropriately according to a person's exalted workings.

Reading the signals of the energy of an attacker allows appropriate response to the movement of an attack. In daily life as well, paying attention means recognizing the signals as guidance toward alignment with change. There are always signals, but when we are distracted with "more important things," the little bumps and oil lights along the way go unnoticed, ignored, or worse, disregarded. An "out of it" mindset can mistake failure to listen for persistence and determination. If we are pushed out of connection by the rush, the signals then irritate an already overloaded system. The potential value of any information is diminished or lost altogether.

Some signals are critically more important than others. Nonetheless, every little disturbance, warning, or alarm signal is a message from the universal intelligence that designed the alive system. Being alert to and watching for signals as simple as increasing volume in voice, or increasing muscular tension in any situation, triggers the system's automatic self-correcting process. Missing the signals potentially ends in problems that, in the quantum world of Aiki, dissolve into unformed potential available to be focused through intent.

The subtle art means awakening to focusing attention on the signals, the subtle whisperings always a reminder to "return to source." The ability to choose a state pivots on attention repositioning its location with each pulse of vitality. Through "listening" when the energy flows, we allow the messages of the signals to get through and to be heard, considered, and acted upon. Developing the ability to hear and respond to signals allows attention to notice sooner and correct faster.

CENTERING

Centering is the term applied to self-reflexively responding to the signals that call attention back into a centered and balanced relationship in each dimension. Centering, as an action toward a quality of being, describes an ongoing process. The energy field aligns attention or state of being with center in each aspect: psyche, soma, corpus. When we enter the vitality of self, magnetic radiance increases as attention moves into the center of the central core.

Centering begins in the physical dimension because it is accessible and tangible. While attention is paid to feeling, balance is the natural state. In good balance, the body functions well in the physical dimension. Capability diminishes when one is off-balance physically, because holding one's position requires a tensing of counterbalancing muscles. The system can't fully pay attention to anything else until balance corrects, thus freeing energy for direction by intent. This holds true in the mental and emotional realms as well as in the realm of the spirit. Unifying center and balance in each realm, spirit magnetizes true north.

To center is to transform function. Physically, in the martial arts, loss of center or balance means a loss of power. Improved balance enhances power. Tension and relaxation in balance produce an effective tone in the realm of kinesthetic movement. Centered and balanced, one can deliver more power to a throw or strike and is less vulnerable to either. When off-balance, the reverse is true.

Power derives from the ongoing ability to correct balance, a fact that is dramatically true in a martial situation but equally valuable in every facet of life. Through repetition, centering builds synaptic pathways that activate returning to one's best operating place, in motion and in the moment, while activating function in the external world.

The alive system, as it focuses the light of attention into experiencing, automatically turns on the self-reflexive process of correction. When listened to, any signals encouraging a realignment of the quality of participation activate an encompassing, proprioceptive system. Self-correction is the natural state of a self-reflexive alive system, except and until attention gets lost or distracted. Then, signals get missed.

Training in how to use the principles while responding to an attack develops the ability to return to center when it is most needed, under pressure. Flexibility, speed, and power, decisive qualities in the martial realm, translate to response ability in the mental and emotional realms. When energy is expended in tension that is compounded by the resistance it creates, it debilitates function, whether we are innovating physical movement in the face of an attack, or opening our spirit to inquiry.

Centering describes the ongoing process of aligning the subtle facets that so invisibly yet so dramatically affect life. Aligning, allowing, and appreciating frees energy, increasing speed, power, and precision in physical action. It is a way of reintroducing the finer aspects to each other as an interconnected, interpenetrating system. The realms of thought and feeling exist in a finer dimension. Their influence is stronger and subtler, easier to miss, and requires a high degree of self-reflexivity. Osensei's process works equally well in every dimension. Refining balance changes the potential of the field in every realm.

Center balances and includes the totality so completely that the functional story becomes that of one system, potentially transforming the field of conflict to one of confluence. Mentally, center balances differing ideas, seeing beyond a classical point of view to a balanced understanding of a story's relativity. Considering the complexity of multiple known as well as unknown factors at play in any situation opens creativity's channel.

Through translating the principles of center and balance into the realm of the spirit, center and balance make one less susceptible to being influenced to act against the voice of inner guidance. Attuning to the quality of engagement, balance keeps attention from getting so ethereal it can't function effectively, or so concrete as to lose the ability to dream and imagine.

Feeling stuck, tight, or "out of it" are signals along the highway of life indicating guidance that leads back to center. Blame, which focuses on circle losing touch with center, can be read as a signal. If central core is weak or attention disconnects from it, external projections will be taken as stories to be believed. A reinforcing cycle then projects attention further from connecting with central core, and the cycle accelerates.

Self-reflexivity returns experience to source, energizing attention's power. It may not seem to immediately address the issue needing to change . . . at first. But it does change the way one participates in the situation, which affects the unfolding.

LOCATION: THE ENERGY CONTINUUM

Some days seem better than other days. Though one is still oneself, "feeling" changes day to day, in every situation. Feeling better, aligning the somatic focus of attention into experiencing Ki, brings forth a vibrant state of being. When we radiate positive Ki, things seem to go well. When things seem to go well, it seems like a good day. Days of less permeability between Ki and conscious attention, which entrench rather than dissolve the frame of identity, don't go as well. Feeling colors the kind of day and quality of days pouring into the future. Days run into . . . lives.

On one end of the continuum, feeling lives in the glow of life with the pure joy of an infant. On the other, under pressure from the same life energy, resistance to the energy builds to the point where stress becomes distress.

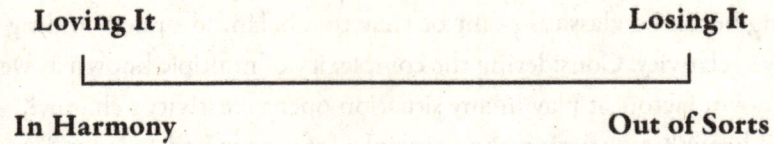

Loving It		Losing It
In Harmony		**Out of Sorts**

Nadeau Sensei said, "Think about a fair day, a good day. Every now and then we have a great day. Wow, why can't every day be like that?" Centering moves state toward the experience described as a "good day." To illustrate, see figures 1, 2, and 3.

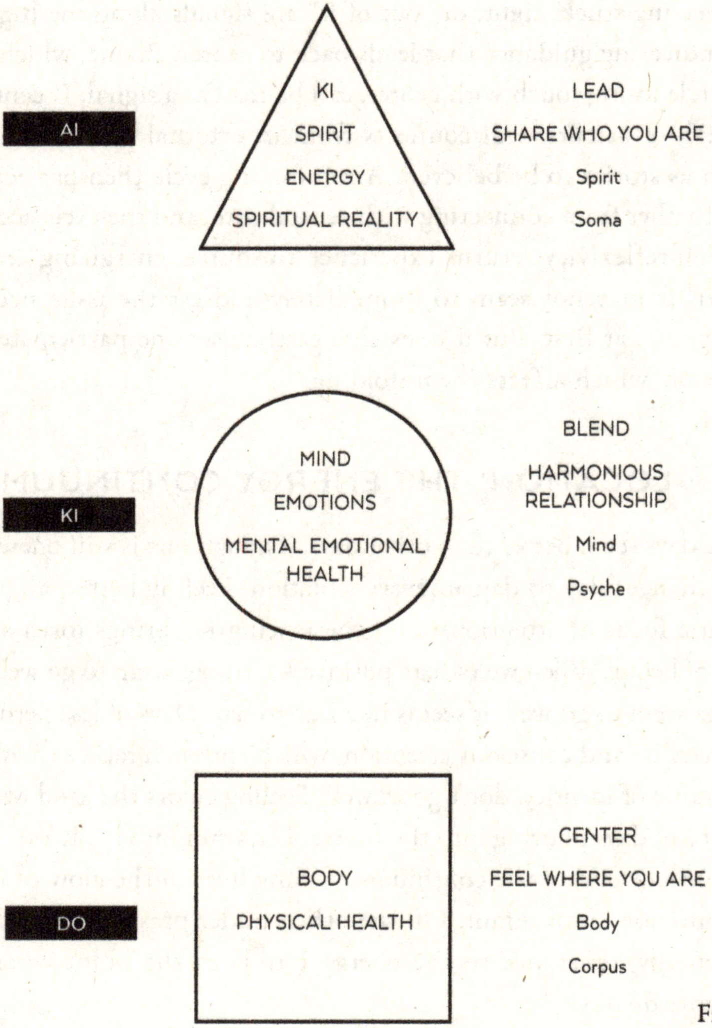

AI

KI
SPIRIT
ENERGY
SPIRITUAL REALITY

LEAD
SHARE WHO YOU ARE
Spirit
Soma

KI

MIND
EMOTIONS
MENTAL EMOTIONAL
HEALTH

BLEND
HARMONIOUS
RELATIONSHIP
Mind
Psyche

DO

BODY
PHYSICAL HEALTH

CENTER
FEEL WHERE YOU ARE
Body
Corpus

Fig. 1

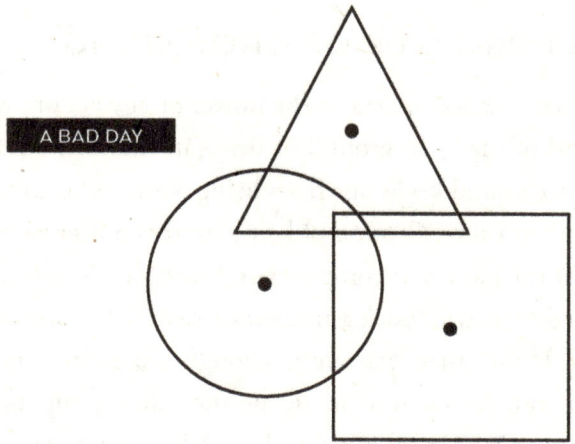

Fig. 2

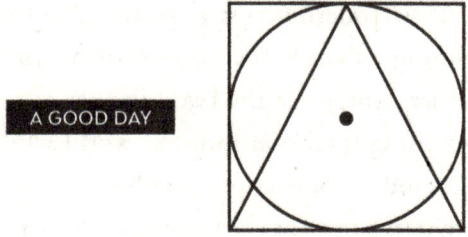

Fig. 3

A "good day" occurs to the degree that the life energy, or center, merges with conscious experience, or circle, expanding exploration into the unified field experience. Centered, grounded, and flowing offers a better place to operate from than feeling out of sorts. The spiritual journey into center only takes a moment, and it gets faster with practice.

When we center ourselves physically, the skeletal structure supports the body, and the musculature naturally relaxes. Because being is a unified field, when the body relaxes, the mind and emotions relax as well, making physical moves easier and spiritual presence brighter. Adjusting attitude, and centering spiritually, allow ground of being to support the expression and experience of aliveness.

THE PRINCIPLE OF GROUNDING

Increasing ground connection increases the power of any action, whether the physical ground of earth, or ground of being in the spiritual dimensions. Connection to ground keeps one from being blown off course, as the keel and rudder do for a ship. Ground of being sources power to continually find and follow the path that completes and fulfils life's unfolding.

Receiving a slight electric shock stimulates a rush. The force is generally upward rising. If the current is strong enough, the hair on the body literally stands on end. At the next level, the shoulders go up and heels come off the ground. One step further and it's debilitating. Any further than that, and it's terminal. Ground effectively handles energy in a functional path. When experienced from a balanced state, the energy, instead of being upsetting, becomes enlivening and increases capability.

Grounding is more than surrendering, just as getting comfortable is more than relaxing. Grounding balances the upward-rising and downward-sinking forces, so that we experience the two together as polarities in the force field of life. Focusing intention into the world while relaxing the whole system into grounded connection gives birth to magic that comes only from unification, doing both at the same time. When the two forces are experienced as a unified field, aliveness functions in relationship to the whole. Aligning the domains activates the dimensional shift. As they align, power increases. With the radiant glow of Ki comes a spirit of engagement, a confidence, an inner calmness, a universal listening.

When we consider the power of harmony, a recurrent theme is that resistance impedes flow and diminishes power and capability. Resistance limits possibility, whether the flow of electrons along neural currents, high speed precision, physical movements, or spiritual powers of imagination and creativity. Aikido aligns with and intentionally utilizes both the internal and the external energy of a situation. Aikido loves resistance, and its love transforms that resistance into flow, absorbing and applying the originating energy to create precision performance and positive resolution.

Being stuck in past thoughts and beliefs engenders limited creativity. Sensing no options, reactivity collapses into fear. Resistance reactively tightens defensively and assembles a world that defends knowledge and beliefs against any new or challenging information, ideas, or thoughts. Without using practice to develop the power of letting go and not knowing, creativity is blocked by holding to the known.

A disconnected state loses power, and a constricted one is likely to alternate between resistance and explosive cycles of avoiding, misusing, and abusing power. Default behavior, from frustration and rudeness to physical violence, signals resistance to experience, disconnecting from creative possibility.

The potential energy buildup that occurs from not listening to the power and possibilities that creativity is offering can create a quantum leap or dimensional shift in the wrong direction. Violence emanates out of contained energy, when creativity is what is needed. When the aspects of being are fragmented, people interact incoherently, "scared out of their wits." The gravity of grounding reassembles the shattered fragments to allow remembering of the original unified field experience.

An ungrounded state of being turns the energy commonly labeled as fear into the out-of-control outbursts of anger and aggression that have colored so much of human history. Whereas when energy flows in the feeling of confidence, it produces an open presence. Connected to a sense of power, one is less likely to default to defensive or aggressive behavior. A centered-grounded state of being handles power in a perceptive, aligned, and appropriate manner. Calming the spirit and returning to source empowers listening, and intelligent adaptation to change.

When connected to central ground of being, one's inner harmony is less disturbed by any aspect of experience. Proper alignment generates more than sufficient energy, engendering generosity and the resonant, reciprocating echoes. Grounding the past and connecting to the emerging universe produce direct experience of the energy of the moment. Balance and alignment make grounding an option even during action or while under pressure. Attending to visceral experience allows the alive system to hear the signals and listen, meaning translate and apply the messages informing and guiding life along a grounded path.

In a grounded, present state, participating in the flow of change, Aikido responds harmoniously to whatever happens in the unfolding. Without any preset on how life should happen, there's no break in the unified field. Without preconception about how creation should unfold, one can influence the whole while blending with it, "both at the same time." Aikido finds its path through blending: first internally centering, blending attention into vitality and creating the strong force; then blending with the subtle force through change, through a situation, through interaction in the world. The signals and messages guide a path that unfolds naturally. There is no resistance, as following gravity is a river's bestowed mission.

Art and science seek a state of openness, a pure, unimpeded experience of creative force. Ground establishes a sense of confidence, a base for the expression of positive Ki. Each pulse, releasing tension into inquiry both in the musculature and belief systems, releases holding the musculature in a previously adopted physical posture. Ground allows letting go of prejudices because it is stable in itself; ground has no need to hold onto them.

THE VALUE OF NOTHING

The structure of a home is important because the emptiness inside a house creates space for life. Grounding in a place of nothing brings forth a dynamic field, useful in its emptiness. When we enter into the moment empty of pre-set conclusions, the universe is experienced as it is. Appearing as nothing, the shining void, a field of potential emptiness, propagates infinite innovative synaptic connections.

When upward rising and downward sinking are in balance, it is as if there were nothing. The practice of nothing develops the ability to let form generate spontaneously, drawing from experience yet free of restrictions from neural connections based in the past. A state of fluid emptiness in the face of any challenge or required action provides the space that gives birth to innovation in strategy, tactics, and technique. Absent any preset, solutions develop that are uniquely appropriate to a given situation, spontaneously, seemingly out of nothing.

Grounding is not erasing the past. Letting go doesn't mean losing memories and knowledge. Rather it means dissolving the hold previous neural pathways tend to put on presence and creativity. Intentionally experiencing the two forces as one allows using the known rather than inattentively succumbing to its containment. To experientially feel self as a unified field of both forces at the same time means to critically distinguish the concept of grounding emotions from that of trying to repress or avoid them.

As we ground physical weight into the Earth, our musculature relaxes. Grounding in the emotional realm allows letting go of fixation on the past while yet retaining any value it offers. Presence releases the naturally expansive nature of awareness, creating an increasingly permeable state of being that empowers us to respond through improvisation, creatively and innovatively new again at each instant.

The power of not knowing enters the future in a pure and open spirit. A spirit of harmony dissolves form and knowing in interactive evolution at each moment, even as the moment changes. Surrendering the known into nothing is the power of the sage. It is why their wisdom seems so unfathomable. *Nothing* has no limitation.

IRIMI-KOKYU: IN AND WITH

ENJOYING JOINING THE UNKNOWN

The Japanese word *irimi* translates as "entering." *Kokyu* is translated most commonly as "breath," and implies joining or blending. Irimi-kokyu means participating "in and with," engaging "in" and aligning "with" the unfolding of each universal pulse. This concept is often written as *irimi-tenkan*, which translates as "entering and turning," and though this translation is accurate, "entering and joining" aligns more with the feeling of the intended outcome.

In the physical art of Aikido, irimi describes entering "off the line" of the attack into a position beside, aligned with, and slightly behind an attacker—a positive joining, entering without opposing. When we operate from the value of nothing, entering the vacant space allows us to influence the expression of the energy, whether a physical attack or by embracing change without resistance.

A non-confrontational, aligned position enhances the field, influencing the source that powers the attack and increasing the potential for resolution. Irimi goes beyond the physical and implies positive entry *in and with* the mental, emotional, and spiritual dimensions. Irimi-kokyu means entering the moment *in and with* full engagement.

When a threat is perceived, the body reactively tightens, hardening itself in defensive reaction. Though condensing musculature can be a strategic defense to minimize injury from impact, withdrawing energy, awareness, and perception from engagement in a situation diminishes effectiveness. Contraction and withdrawal of Ki reduce muscular speed, strength, and range of motion in the physical realm, as well as thinking's facility and clarity in dealing with a challenge or resolving a situation.

Resistance to experience, and withdrawing attention, diminish influence. Using skiing as an analogy, the power of irimi is fundamental to influencing adjustment of the angle of the skis. Controlling momentum and slowing speed require turning perpendicular to the downhill direction and the momentum of gravity. Body movement communicates direction to the skis through the transfer of mass. Pressing weight into the skis communicates the intended direction through the body's momentum. The body's weight on the skis gives intent the power to implement turning the skis.

As our speed increases, the reflexive response mistakenly pulls away from the source of power that is increasing momentum, in this case gravity. Yet leaning back away from the accelerating speed pulls our weight back and out of the skis. Without the engagement of body mass, it is impossible to communicate intent to the skis and control the direction. Instead, leaning back communicates to the skis to go faster, reinforcing the desire to pull back. Holding back from a situation diminishes influence, so that we require greater effort to have any effect, and it becomes potentially impossible to accomplish a desired goal.

To influence the skis requires experientially entering into the momentum, the downhill motion, wholly and totally, with full body, mind, and spirit. Entering into the center, the heart of the source that stimulates reactivity, is a demonstration of courage. It is also harmonious. It is also intelligent. Pressing weight into connection with the skis, and *into and with* the increasing force of gravity, functionally delivers the skier's intention to turn.

Entering the experience, leaning forward into the momentum, and engaging the mass of body weight into the skis, communicates a skier's intention to turn, controlling the direction and thereby the speed. Irimi— entering the situation—creates the unity of the skier with the skis, allowing them to function together as a system. Then intention has power to turn, and the skis get the message; the skier can turn and control their speed to any degree they wish. Entering into the momentum, unifying the field, allows intention to produce action, influencing a desired outcome.

Irimi, entering *into and with* experience, is the realm of power. Resistance to engaging diminishes influence, increases the cycle of resistance, and leads into fear, further reducing influence and effectiveness. The way to fulfill the challenge of life is to "enter," to bravely engage energetic awareness into whatever unfolding experience the gods offer. Irimi implies first connecting attention *in and with* experience. To enter into the experience of life—intentionally, positively, self-reflexively, and wholeheartedly— increases personal power, transforming reactivity into creativity.

In skiing, the rush and the potential reactive avoidance of the energy both increase with faster momentum. In business, the rush increases in direct proportion to the dollar amount at risk. And in personal relationships, reactivity increases in proportion to the degree of caring or emotional charge.

Entering is the path to influence. To drive a car, one would naturally enter by taking up one's position in the driver's seat—far and away the best position to take when driving. Connecting to attention and centering into experience is the way to put the driver in the driver's seat.

ENTERING OFF THE LINE

In Aikido, a basic harmonious response is entering off the line of an attack, out of the way of any oncoming threat. Getting off the line does not mean avoiding an experience. It means making a harmonious, intelligent response in anticipation of WIGO, much like getting out of the way of an oncoming car, or allowing someone else to express what they think or feel. Creating a harmonious relationship is an intelligent response.

Entering off the line allows the practitioner to guide the attacker's center, potentially neutralizing future attack. Aikido blends with energy in its original state, where influence is greatest, thus opening creative possibility. The application in Aikido of moving *into and with*, entering while maintaining harmonious relationship, comes forth out of the magic of unification: $1 + 1 = 1$.

By obliquely entering "off the line of attack," a practitioner connects with the question behind the statement of an attacker. The act of entering an experience, as discomfort seemingly pushes attention away from the intensity of vitality, is irimi. It implies attention's entry *into and with* experiencing a situation, to effectively predict potential, design strategy, and execute action. Entering off the line, respecting the expression of force, increases influence. Entering in the spirit of harmony produces confluence.

EXTRAORDINARY LISTENING

In the physical metaphor, Aikido adopts a non-resistant relationship to an attack through joining with it. In the verbal, mental, and emotional realms, "off the line" implies not taking someone's words or attitude personally as an attack, even if intended that way. A spirit of peaceful reconciliation seeks to understand the motivation that is engendering an assault, to understand the force driving the behavior.

Defensiveness indicates the need to move off the line. Identity, when it believes in itself, defends against the force of change instead of harmonizing with it. The shift from identity's defensiveness to the self-reflexivity of the unified field opens the possibilities of learning to see in new ways, and of innovating potential creative response. Moving emotionally off the line is the opposite of not hearing: it allows us to hear the meaning of a stated issue, and the activating needs behind it, out of the way of the tonality of affect with which it may be delivered. As identity dissolves into the vitality of self, connection and understanding listen.

If one enters in beside an attacker in the physical world, this action translates in the realm of communication as trying to see things from another person's point of view. It brings forth positively receptive communication cycles, instead of the ever-escalating defensive, aggressive, or contentious behavior that disagreement reinforces. Aligning with energy as information generates harmonious relationship and positive spirit.

GOING WITH THE FLOW

Everyone who comes in to study Aikido already knows the phrase "go with the flow," which seems like a commonsense idea. Yet living in the quantum world, it is and it isn't. In the same way that *comfortable* doesn't just mean *relaxing* but includes blending, sinking, and opening to the excitation, going with the flow neither means giving up to the flow nor being pushed around by the flow, nor does it mean passivity, hanging out around the flow. That would be a misunderstanding where people hear "with the flow" but seem to miss the "go" part. *Going* with the flow, entering into and participating in unfolding experience, is in every sense an engaged, intentional practice of positive spirit.

Harmonious non-resistance is a very positive form of engagement, an attitude of learning and creativity, of entry into experience beyond the known. The superposition of nonresistance means actively adding a note to create the harmony. Just as one voice sings alongside another in perfect harmony, without dissonance, dominance, or resistance, a harmonious relationship influences change, enriching creativity and enhancing the outcome without opposing the moment.

Going with the flow may or may not involve active participation or generating action. Engaging *in and with* means being participatory and response able, engaged and harmonious, regardless of the appearance of success or lack thereof. Entering into harmonious relationship creates a unified field. Then universal harmony naturally influences the outcome.

Knowing that exercise is good is one thing. Actually exercising is an entirely different thing. It's one thing to know that no one is as clearheaded or effective when upset. It's another thing altogether to recognize this and take responsibility for it when upset. Doing so under pressure in a critical situation, when emotions and hormones surge, requires a finer dimension of presence then is commonly developed in the current state of human consciousness—because having the knowledge and turning that knowledge into experiential power are two different things.

KOKYU: HARMONIOUS RELATIONSHIP WITH THE BREATH OF LIFE

The Japanese word *kokyu* is older than the word *Aiki*. It is a fundamental and vital concept in the art of Aikido. Kokyu, so fundamental in its application and so diverse in its use, is an essential concept in that it gives Aikido its power. The word *kokyu* is commonly translated as "breath," or in the martial sphere as "breath power." Kokyu also implies several other meanings that have important implications for the study.

Life pivots on

    the focus of intent,

        the harmony of the breath,

            the location of attention.

Enjoy

    breathing

        aliveness.

            It's Your Art Now.

Kokyu describes when forces unify in harmony; both are present, yet their differences blend them into one, and they enrich each other as well as the field they constitute and express. Harmonious unification is when the three realms described in Shinto mythology—the manifest, the hidden, and the divine—harmonize, blend, and unify as one. When there is no struggle between forces, when any tension between them resolves into charmed enjoyment of each other toward a positive outcome, that is kokyu.

Kokyu, also meaning "blending into harmony," describes a state where things function together harmoniously. When people are very good friends, get along well, or work well together, they are said to have good kokyu. When people sing together in harmony, they are said to have good kokyu. When the unique tones of beautiful voices meld, creating an increased richness of sound, that is kokyu.

To use music as a metaphor, in tune, in time, and in balance the unified field of sounds blends into one. As each tone, still an individual sound, dissolves, blending into a unified vibrational experience in the singers and the listeners, that is kokyu.

Kokyu lovingly brings forth the harmony of Ai. Yet the concept of harmony only begins to define kokyu. Kokyu also includes the process of joining in, so it also implies irimi. Kokyu as harmony includes qualities of adaptability, fluidity, unification, and resonance. Understanding of the concept can be expanded and enriched through each of those windows.

The words *harmony* and *arm* both derive from a Greek root meaning "fitting" or "joining," as an arm fits into or joins with the shoulder. Water flows "in" harmony "with" gravity. Trained in harmony, one plays "in" tune "with" the rest of the orchestra. Self-reflexivity in singing means adjusting one's voice *into* the key and *with* the rhythm of the song. When action of virtually any kind in the manifest realm comes out of a fluid blend of tones or qualities of resonant harmony, that is kokyu. In the finer realms, kokyu translates as a harmonious connection with the power that activates the breath, the power that drives and sustains the life force and the whole of creation.

The art of peace defuses the force of an attack by moving with its motion. Fitting into the shape of the motion of an attack increases the receptivity of the initiating force, in the same way listening and understanding soften anger. Energy, when in a spirit of harmonious relationship, fluidly fits and joins, adaptive to change, transforming negative energy into peaceful reconciliation and negative situations into positive options.

Energy, force, and power all merge together in the principle of harmony, along with intelligence and enrichment of experience. Synonyms for harmony include peace, friendship, understanding, unity, accord, coherence, cooperation, tranquility, empathy, sympathy, like-mindedness, meeting of minds, symphony, unanimity, good will, kinship, rapport, affinity, amicability, amity, compatibility, concord, correspondence, consonance, consistency, balance, orchestration, proportion, symmetry, and consensus. The power of harmony resolves conflict. It should go unsaid that the opposite does the opposite. That this fact is so commonly missed at this point in the development of human knowledge, and more importantly in human behavior, is a key element in human tragedy.

People do know this, as a mutable aspect of the mysterious story. But in the heat of the rush, the brain's higher functions yield to the reptilian reactivity of the basal ganglia. Tremendous focus is required for this reactivity to be mediated by the thoughtfulness of the cortex. With training, we can respond from a unified field rather than reacting from fragments, and this response becomes a positive synaptic pathway.

The effort required to develop pathways honoring the cerebral and frontal lobes of the brain, opening possibilities of peaceful and creative dialogue, seems to be a greater effort than the endless wars for peace. The challenge is that war urgently and immediately demands and consumes investment. Peace requires investment *in advance*. When we consider the difference in value and outcome, it seems as if the equation was never calculated. Human consciousness has a moving average and struggles with being asleep at the wheel. Or we've come too recently out of the caves to see in the sunlight . . . yet.

Harmonious relationship with Ki allows the energy of the life force to flow freely, intelligently. It defines unification, letting us heal into wholeness internally while it appears as harmonious relationship externally. The power of intelligent harmony in one's life will ripple outward with dramatically greater effects in the interaction of the species. While the higher aspects of brain development have taken place in most people, they must be activated to be realized, as an apple must be eaten to be assimilated. Repeatedly returning to *feeling into* experience takes growth and development through a dimensional shift into a field of infinite potential.

In the personal realm, kokyu is an experience of inner peace that expands into a dynamic discovery of becoming. Harmony enriches aliveness, moving feeling awareness toward a sense of well-being. An emotional dynamic, a feeling, and a tension urge feeling toward the totality of being, entrainment with all. The power of kokyu extends the resonance and reciprocating echoes of inner harmony out into the world.

Kokyu is neither surrender nor domination but respects a diversity of universal manifestation in a spirit of learning. Harmonizing, blending, and unifying with the mystery causes art, technical form, and technique to appear that have never been seen before. Artistic creativity does not conform to understanding of the past. The unknown is the doorway into what is becoming. Artistic imagination, spontaneous infinite creativity, leads the future into the present.

Aiki kokyu is harmonious interpenetration of the spiritual, permeating the physical as one voice. Kokyu describes the feeling of radiance that resonates through our system when our breathing moves in conscious harmony with the pulse of the universe. When the rhythm of breathing echoes the impulse that activates the breath, that is kokyu.

Aligning the intentional and autonomic aspects of breathing into a unified field is the active, fundamental practice that connects attention with experience. Presence increases through kokyu, connecting the conscious breath with the autonomic breath in harmonious relationship. Consciously breathing by listening to the impulse to breathe, unites both in remembering experientially that they exist in the larger sphere as one system.

THE PULSE OF THE UNIVERSAL BREATH

A beginner walks into the dojo aware, if asked, that they breathe, but rarely aware of their breathing. As a practitioner advances, developing sensitivity to the finer dimensions of sensation and sensory awareness, the impulse to breathe surfaces into conscious awareness. Harmony with the pulse of energy of the universal breath can breathe wisdom into life.

As the student advances, they are introduced to the multiple phases and cycles of breathing.

Breathing the Whole System

1. *External breathing*: Air moves in and out of the lungs.
2. *Transfer*: Oxygen is absorbed into the bloodstream.
3. *Transport*: Blood carries oxygen to every cell.
4. *Absorb*: Every cell absorbs oxygen.
5. *Burn*: Each cell lives, burning oxygen into aliveness, the glow of life itself.

Oxygen saturation, distinct from surplus or deficit, allows the burning of aliveness into life. Every cell of the body that is in perfect harmony with its oxygen exchange gives off a radiance. Attention glows with the sensation of oxygen burning into joyful aliveness. The phases of the breath in symphonic resonance activate each cell into glowing as its most charming, enjoyable self.

The cellular oxygenation balance burns oxygen into life, and it effects emotional balance in the spiritual realm, and vice versa. As with any band or orchestra, if the cycles of breathing practice together, the music comes together as one system, one sound, one vibrational experience. The result is that the unified field assembles as if it suddenly remembers itself.

When kokyu's harmony cultivates the spirit of reconciliation, this constitutes the essence of Aikido practice. In a martial situation, that spirit would give birth to Aikido techniques. In every other realm of existence, it would produce techniques appropriate to those realms.

Blending, adaptability, fluidity, resonance, and unification, all facets of the diamond of kokyu, reflect a single source, Ichi Rei. Each of these qualities contributes a slightly different angle of approach toward the overarching, yet fundamental concept embodied in the word *kokyu*, the central tributary of the art of Aikido.

A cycle fulfills and an exceptional gift of kokyu occurs when someone is listened to enough to feel complete—when they feel heard to the point where they exhaust everything, until they have nothing left to say; when the energy pushing them to speak drops and relaxation signals a sense of being complete in the communication. A sense of fulfillment in having been heard and understood radiates, and the energy they emanate indicates their interest in listening.

When someone is listened to in that way, it bends time-space, and the world changes. The way of harmony listens in this same way to the shape of the energy of an attacker. Likewise, the art of peace listens to the impulse to breathe. Aikido listens to the creative force of the universe.

A RIVER FLOWS TO THE SEA

The quality of spirit in the first nanosecond of entry into any engagement is the seed crystal of experience. Entering into a negotiation in a spirit of litigation presets the win-lose frame of a sword fight. As a seed crystal, it sets in motion reciprocating echoes that generally produce the outcome expected.

When we encounter even wisps of a contentious tone in a negotiating partner, billions of years of reactive evolution are already activating long before words are spoken and ideas are generated. It is into that field of energy that a conversation ensues. Synaptic patterning with its attendant systems of thought and belief establishes a "mind set," a field of thought energy that influences the unfolding before action has begun.

Hijacked by the amygdala, reactivity responds defensively, turning conversations into discussions and discussions into arguments that quickly avalanche into a win-lose, zero sum tonality. Collegiality dies, as does any beauty of synergy it might potentially offer, while energy is channeled in the opposite direction. A different set of reciprocating echoes comes into play.

Resistance to Ki shows up as a tightening in the body-mind, draining energy and effectiveness. Resistance to life's energy blocks creativity, resulting in a victim state of mind, which engenders negative thoughts and perceptions. Commonly in the negotiation story, like in every other domain, fear turns to aggression. The rush drives a desire to convince, disguised as clarity and commitment yet concealing a defensive failure to listen. Then, instead of meeting in a spirit of what can be learned and what are the possibilities for peaceful resolution, the parties involved fall into negative creativity, emphasizing any conflict while distracting attention away from areas of agreement.

A field of infinite potential collapses into fight-or-flight reactive behavior. To compound the misfortune, neural energy follows and reinforces established pathways. Once it starts, it is hard to stop. The reactivity drains energy in courses of action and thought that could have been applied to creative resolution, could have been used to create a beautiful world. Starting off on the wrong tack causes us to end up where no one really wants to be.

Whether negotiating partners work *with* to resolve or instead *against* to prevail is dramatically impacted by the seed crystal at the instant of entry, so mutable, so easily influenced. Creativity and its power come from training our state of being as the basis for action before influencing a situation. This process, which originates in a spirit of harmony, begins by developing the quality of the being who is creating the story.

Reframing the energy rush as excitement, as if meeting a good friend, galvanizes the energy as an ally on entry into any situation. When listening allows someone to complete their communication, an opening occurs. In that prescient moment of receptivity, as yang changes to yin, a single word can generate a feeling that transforms the tonality of experience. Shifting into a state that is likely to generate a good story at that second is life changing.

At first blush, it is nearly impossible to fully comprehend the incredible power of entering every moment of life in a balanced, grounded state, in contrast to the cost of not doing so. A tone of positive spirit, by radiating positive intent, sets in motion reciprocating echoes. Once we can enter any negotiation in a spirit of harmony, the echoes engender an exploration toward understanding. Listening and dialogue produce a field of potential innovative, magnetizing solutions. A river of confluence winds its way to the sea of peaceful reconciliation.

Often in negotiation or mediation, people walk away thinking they have an agreement, when in fact they have two. In such cases, the actual implementation is problematic or never happens. Listening into a unified field of agreement allows the two parties to leave in actual confluence. This type of listening represents seeking understanding instead of arguing specifics, right or wrong, language and outcomes. Treating the cause rather than the symptoms resolves the needs that drive the demands, and thus creates peace, not a temporary ceasefire.

This doesn't mean that the solution lies exactly in the middle. A surfer or windsurfer leans into the momentum needed to direct the board and enhance the ride; they do so out of the unified field experience. Peaceful reconciliation recognizes the oneness of the universal system, allowing each aspect of the system expression and inclusion. Favoring a solution that leans more in one direction than another comes out of feeling the whole and reconciling all the forces at play. The power of kokyu—blending, fluidly adapting, and unifying in a spirit of resonance, love, and harmony—brings forth spontaneous innovation.

Peaceful reconciliation, or the failure to achieve it, impacts life dramatically when conflict occurs with a family member, a neighbor, or a coworker. In close relationships or ongoing ones, resolving conflict without injury to either party enhances the ability to live or work together in the spirit of harmony. Cooperation, powered by love and harmony, allows society to focus its collective creativity to overcome challenges.

Centering continually returns attention to connection with the source of its power, reconciling the discord and calming the spirit. Returning to source heals any reactive drive to dictate the behavior and beliefs of others. To paraphrase the Buddha, "Those who understand this enter every situation in a positive spirit of peaceful reconciliation. Those who don't, suffer." It follows that they also cause suffering, which sets in motion reciprocating echoes, world without end.

Ai means both harmony and love. Aiki, in the conversation of human relationship, makes possible listening and adapting in loving harmony with any input, whether complementary or critical. Aligning in a preferred relationship with a changing universe, moving harmoniously, reconciles threatening energy into free energy and change into opportunity. The power of harmonious spirit makes listening possible, affecting every realm and every dimension.

The eternal battle for peace takes place internally, within one's understanding and experience. The experience of vitality draws attention into and through a portal opening to the totality of the universe. For an individual, that experience begins with central core, with resolving internal discord. Peace within leads to peace without.

Study and practice of the art of Aikido transforms spontaneous, infinite creativity from being merely an occasional thought or occurrence, to a way of life. When the founder spoke of harmonizing with the energy of the universe, he also indicated that everyone must discover a personal path to harmony. The first step, winning over the discord within one's own mind, begins with entering into experience harmoniously. The holy war is an inside job

UNIFICATION AND RESONANCE: THE MUSIC OF THE SPHERES

Harmony in music is the blending of simultaneous sounds of different pitch or quality, making chords, units, or fields of harmony. A choir sings different parts, which come together in a harmonious relationship. In a symphony orchestra, the instruments produce unified sections, and the sounds of the sections unify in concert. A harmonious musical relationship is one that enriches the overtone series of two or more sounds, increasing the power of their effect. The magic of an enriched overtone series activates in the emotional realm of the listener. The "field" of music is created through kokyu—harmony, blending, and unification.

The unity of voices in music is not an either/or. It is a both/and. In music, functioning as a supportive couple, masculine and feminine voices unify in resonance to enrich the total sound. Blending two ways of looking at reality offers potential enrichment to life, as two voices that blend well enrich the overtone series and the joy of anyone listening.

The occurrence of two notes at the same time, in harmony, creates a field of resonance. As sound waves merge, they interact, canceling and reinforcing aspects of each other. The slightest variance in either timbre or pitch affects the quality of the sound, as does the balance of volume. The richness of the sound changes according to the relationship of the notes, altering the feeling that the listener experiences.

Music comes forth as dynamic tension that releases into increasing harmony. It creates a resonance, reminding and reconnecting the feeling experience with the awe of its own vastness. Experience is mutable as tuning an instrument or changing the notes in a musical composition. Change emotional overtones between people, and a similar resonant process occurs. The choice to enter each moment in positive spirit energy dynamically enriches the overtone series of the universal symphony.

UNIFYING RESONANCE: BLENDING INTO ONENESS

The basic practice of *in and with* combines the two basic principles of irimi and kokyu. *In and with* implies harmonious relationship. It begins with presence, the viscerally felt experience of participating *in and with* creation. The idea is simple. Yet when it comes to execution, the difficulty is that both *in and with* must be done in the same time-space, not one and then the other. Both "in"—meaning engaged, present, and attentive—and "with," meaning blending in a positive, joyful spirit, occur at the same time.

Something as simple as screwing a light bulb into a socket demonstrates the principle of combining two forces and the power of unification. To screw in a light bulb, it must be inserted and turned at the same time, both at once, or it doesn't engage. *In and with* blends both forces in the same time-space. Unification is a both/and that produces the magic of function.

Ironically enough, the sword, thought of as cutting things apart, simultaneously offers a counterintuitive metaphor for the power of unification. A sword cuts because the two sides of the sword become one at the cutting edge. A master sharpens the blade edge to that one molecule that is at once both sides and/or neither. The cutting edge represents the domain where two aspects unify into one, $1 + 1 = 1$, producing the sword's power.

To the degree that mind and body separate, they limit the ability of essence—or spirit—to create or express. As aspects of being lose touch with their unity, power to fulfill and enhance life experience diminishes. Power emanates from unification. When the thresholds of the known and the unknown realms touch, coming together as that one molecule of learning that is at once both the known and the unknown, and/or neither, the unification produces the cutting edge of knowledge, leading change in a spirit of growth and development. Aikido's power enhances life through unifying the manifest and the divine, the known and the unknown realms in the experiential now.

APPLIED HARMONY

Leadership goes beyond "how it is," which, by the time perception has processed it, has already passed. Growth and development, rather, implies entering and learning to lead the target. Successful leadership can be defined as the ability to unify, develop, and guide a family, a team, a company, or a society, merging exploration *into and with* "what is becoming."

Mastery in business means exerting influence through leading the market. Mastery in the business of living works in harmony with the forces of change, adapting as fluidly as water, resolving conflict into confluence. A leader with gravity in any field, by entering into and blending with situations in a positive spirit with intent to produce positive outcomes, in effect curves time-space toward a harmonious universe and a beautiful world.

The power of harmony enriches the beauty of life. A coherent, positive spirit makes an intelligent, useful practice and a beautifully enriching path, rather than reinforcing a fragmented, negative attitude or story. Energy, force, attention, affect, and intelligence all merge together in the principle of kokyu's harmony, putting power in service of spirit.

7

JOY: THE WAY
OF THE WARRIOR

Osensei's

Aikido in Three Easy Lessons

"Love gives birth to harmony.

    Harmony brings forth joy.

        Joy is the greatest treasure.

If one has a benevolent heart, one can give love.

    From love arises harmony,

        and harmony gives birth to happiness.

        Happiness and joy are the greatest treasures.

        The treasure is not gold or diamonds.

        It is spiritual."

—WORDS OF THE FOUNDER

KOKYU NAGÉ

An array of Aikido techniques taught are called Kokyu Nagé. *Nagé* means "to throw" or "one who throws." The term *kokyu* is commonly translated as "breath," and Kokyu Nagé is frequently rendered in English as "breath power throw," though the concept remains generally undefined. Kokyu Nagé describes in essence any action that comes forth out of harmonizing with the pulsing energy that activates the breath. This principle applies to all aspects of life in the energy universe, including beyond the training hall.

Kokyu Nagé in the realm of the spirit means using the power of harmony through blending with the essence of an attacker's life force; it means using the power, energy, and intention that activate vitality, sourced from breath and movement. In daily life, this translates as looking beyond the symptoms or effects and blending with the origin of the energy of change.

When the neutralization or throw comes about with no resistance, that is Kokyu Nagé. As resolution happens without being forced, the relevance of strength evaporates. Harmony, by definition, never contends against force, which the founder taught with the phrase "never defeated means never fighting." Every technique that comes forth of Aiki is Kokyu Nagé birthing infinite forms.

Uniquely, Aikido's philosophy distinguishes neutralizing the attack from neutralizing the attacker. The magic of the art of peace, the power that lets it create a beautiful world, is the inclusion of the intention of protection of the attacker as part of the focus. Transcending life and death, recognizing their oneness with creation, allows consideration of loving protection.

Loving spirit, in turn, sets in motion reciprocating echoes of reconciliation that resonate through the entirety of the manifest realm. Though one's first responsibility is to protect those in one's charge from harm, the spirit of Aikido's teachings also extends the essential attitude of loving protection to the entirety of the universe—for in asking the universe for its protection, we owe it the same in return.

LOVING PROTECTION, PEACEFUL RECONCILIATION

The mission of Aikido, creating a beautiful world, begins internally in experience, harmonizing the polarity between the masculine and feminine, yin and yang forces of energy and attention. Resolving the discord within allows a world to appear where creativity serves joy. By collectively radiating inner peace, we reconcile the world. Kokyu begins in the center of the central core of an individual. It radiates out into the universe to incorporate the mystery.

For people not familiar with Aikido, one of the most difficult concepts to understand is the idea of blending with an attacker. Fighting for survival is a deeply ingrained notion. It formed with the earliest development of the neural processes. The attitude of fighting is based on separation and resistance, on identifying oneself as separate from and in opposition against external forces. Once we are in opposition, conflict escalates, leaving winning or losing as the only options.

If a target moves in exact harmony, blending with the attacking force, it is impossible to deliver the pressure of impact. Moving in harmony diffuses violence and transforms the power of any energy, whatever the quality, whether it is information, pressure, or attack. Impact requires separation and/or resistance. While this fact is easy to see in the physical world, it is subtler in the hidden realm of energy. Yet it is equally true.

Not fighting doesn't mean disengaging. On the contrary, it means increasing engagement and influence through blending. Not forcing does not mean having no strength or power. Rather, *harmony* describes an intelligent use of energy. For instance, when force is used to open a door in the direction it swings, harmony increases power, potential, and creative possibility.

Acceptance here means recognition and moving in concert with WIGO. Harmony doesn't mean passively not producing dissonance.

For harmony to occur, both notes must be sung at the same time. A spiritual warrior sings full body, mind, and spirit.

Like the north and south poles of a magnetic field, the harmony of interpenetrating forces, while identified as two aspects, exists as a unity. So, it is as if, where there were two, there is now one—$1 + 1 = 1$ —leaving nothing to attack or be attacked. The power of Aikido comes from our actively, intentionally participating in and unifying into experiencing the whole of creation as one system.

BLENDING IN TIME

Power comes not only from strength, leverage, or the relationship of position. Unimaginable power can come from a small action at exactly the right time. This happens when tuning in to the intention of an attacker, or to the energy that builds before the attacker crystallizes enough to activate an event. As an analogy for the benefit of catching the action in the stage of formation, consider the ease of changing a set of blueprints compared to changing the structure of a house once it is built.

In Aikido, the blend happens in the hidden dimension as energy gives birth to movement, before action takes form in the visible world. Ai-"Ki" means blending with the "energy of intent" of an attacker. Aikido blends and harmonizes with an attacker's action "a second before," as the action is forming in consciousness—a second before the thought that activates motion can solidify, before neural impulses stimulate the muscular system that creates kinesthetic movement. Aikido blends with the energy of an attack as it's forming in consciousness, before it enters the neural pathways that activate the muscular response, and long before that response activates physical motion.

Osensei demonstrated the power of being able to respond as the idea of the attack forms, inviting a location of attention in the realm of the Kami, the source of creativity. Lest anyone misunderstand this as some abstract, mystical concept, he emphasized repeatedly that the universal force that powers the spirit must flow through the individual, through the physical, and through the body to complete the trinity.

In a spirit of peaceful reconciliation, the oneness of the system unfolds itself. The practice of intentionally entering the moment in warrior's spirit transforms awareness. As the mind opens to re-cognize itself as the whole, identifying as the universe, it finds nothing to resist. The energy of resistance dissolves into flow. As unformed potential, Ki serves intent.

Kokyu makes it possible, through the power of harmony, for systems that are less powerful to affect systems that are more powerful. Challenges that cannot be overcome by force can be led to completion through the power of harmony. Peace is created when yin and yang unify in understanding. Harmoniously balancing the needs of both the individual and the collective is kokyu in the art of civilization, because the collective *is* individuals: both at the same time.

NON-RESISTANCE, ADAPTABILITY, AND FLUIDITY

Irimi kokyu implies entering fluidly, adapting in harmonious spirit, and adjusting in relation to change as it occurs. Water, when it flows, demonstrates non-resistance in its ability to adapt. Water does not wait to start adapting. It is instantaneously and continuously fluid. Water assumes the shape of any container on entry, yet never loses its own nature. Pour it on the ground and it enters every empty space. Water has as its essence a natural fluidity, which allows it to enter the emptiness as the perfect non-resistant yin to every yang. Adapting to change, void of preset, fluidity draws its power from persistence.

Water has a non-resistant relationship with gravity, so its movement is effortless. Water never shrinks from a fall. No matter the terrain, without being taught, water flows downhill. In its natural state a stream flows, filling any pools, and then finds its way onward. Unless it freezes, water never loses its fluidity. Unless it dries up, a river never stops flowing.

Japanese warrior arts grew from the samurai tradition. *Samurai* means "to serve." Water serves thirst, travel, power, and beauty. Water never argues about the shape of things. In the same way, a master martial artist fluidly harmonizes their movements to those of an attacker, fitting them perfectly, neutralizing the energy of the threat, and transforming the field into one of potential resolution. The founder directed us to forge the spirit and thereby enter ever-finer dimensions.

The customer is always right. An ice cream store that serves its customers strawberry when they order chocolate won't stay open long. One never needs to ask for the attention of a good waiter. They anticipate the customer's needs. A waiter who excels knows those needs better than the customer. The magic of service knows when the customer is ready to order, ready for the next course, and ready for the check. Having refined their sensitivity through the balance of circle and center, a master martial artist anticipates and utilizes the energy and action of change. Listening serves their ability to fit into and accommodate the force of an attack, better than the attacker does.

The essential non-resistance of Aikido engages actively, as fluidly as water, in service of the completion of the universe. Harmony, serving the universe what it wants, does not mean giving up in deference to what someone else wants. Harmony in music means the opposite of one note giving up its essence or dominating the other. When two different notes harmonize, they enhance the overtone series of both. That is the power of harmony. In a field of harmony, all the variable resonances unify to enhance the richness of the sound and the experience of everyone who listens.

Moving into a centered, blending, flowing relationship with the force of an attack, changing yin into yang, applies in any domain. To have a harmonious, non-resistant relationship to the energy of life means to learn from the fluid adaptability that water demonstrates.

THE PRINCIPLE OF RESONANCE

Everything is connected to everything. Everything affects everything. Every vibration creates reciprocating echoes affecting everything else. Hit the "D" string on one violin, and if there is another tuned violin in the room, its "D" string will vibrate in resonance. The power of resonance just as easily reinforces dissonance. The principle of resonance creates a change in the field as someone's mood does in a room. Everything affects everything.

Harmony tends to generate harmony, just as hostility tends to generate hostility. Whatever quality radiates into the magnetic field, it will reinforce as well as attract the same kind of energy. A different field of energy will generate different ideas and emotions and attract different partners, jobs, and situations. Each of these will in turn generate another set of reciprocating echoes, resonating with the subtle force, attracting different vibrational colors and tones of the aspects that combine to form the experience of life.

Without understanding or likely even considering the less visible forces at play, a life forms as if it were inevitable destiny. In an energy universe, to change the colors changes the tone, changes the art, changes the symphony. Every change in the quality of attention, attitude, mood, or state of being assembles a different universe.

The biochemical, electromagnetic field of energy connects to, affects, and is affected by everything in the universe. An attitude or quality of spirit, flowing through the magnetic coil that is life at its central core, may at first seem a very subtle tonality. As a focus of attention, it becomes tangible. With practice, intent becomes an art.

DEFCON: REGISTERING DEFENSIVE RESONANCE

The armed forces may not be the first example that comes to mind when we look for models of self-awareness. However, unlike most people, they do have a constant monitoring of how defensively they are postured. They use defensive posture intentionally as a valuable and functional tool.

The U.S. Department of Defense consciously adopts a posture of readiness based on their assessment of the threat of an enemy attack. This is termed their defense readiness condition or "DEFCON." The DEFCON represents the present level of expectation of attack, and the readiness to respond to as well as initiate attack.

During the Cold War, whenever the United States raised their DEFCON, the Soviet Union raised their own classified alert levels, which were less transparent and not as publicly documented as the US system of DEFCON. Whatever the terminology, each stimulated movement in the other and vice versa. This same DEFCON dynamic occurs between people. As people get more defensive, fear leads to aggression, increasing the tendency to attack. So naturally, being around someone who is defensive raises expectancy of an attack, and our DEFCON increases. As one person's defense condition intensifies, it provokes the defense condition of anyone within resonance in an ever-increasing cycle.

The principle of resonance changes one's life with positive or negative effect, as does someone's tone in a room, as does beautiful music or cacophonous noise. Panic and reactivity require no training. They were trained into neural systems since life's evolution began long ago. Reactivity, when resisted, increases defensiveness, and a vicious cycle accelerates. The increase in energy can reach an explosive potential. Any resistance to feeling experience causes pressure to build instead of releasing or freeing the energy into creativity. The same energy, when properly grounded, manifests a field of infinite potential.

Training and practice develop inner gauges that sense levels of defensiveness and conflict with others. Defensiveness, once recognized, is a signal indicating the need to check the instruments and adjust the controls. As the forces unify internally, the ensuing positive spirit of harmony, adaptability, blending, and unification will radiate confidence and lower the DEFCON. Defensiveness creates a reciprocating echo. So does the art of peace.

TAKÉMUSU JIYU WAZA: INFINITE
SPONTANEOUS CREATIVITY—JAZZ

The founder frequently used the term *Takémusu Aiki*, sometimes translated as "kaleidoscopic techniques," implying infinite forms issuing fourth out of harmonious relationship to the creative force.

Také is a term primarily understood as relating to the martial realm, martial studies and skills. *Musu* literally means "to give birth," and like almost every word in the Japanese language, it has subtler implications and encompasses a broad array of concepts. It relates to the realm that gives birth to creativity, infinite or divine realms, the power of creation. The exploration of becoming one with the universe blends attention into the power that brings forms into creation. A creative interpolation might be, the martial art of the gods, or the martial art of divine creation, or infinite creativity.

The reference of Takémusu is that of giving birth to martial skills and, in the larger picture, skills that sustain life. Také can be loosely expanded to reference the realm of capability—extraordinarily effective function in the manifest realm, across all practical skills in the physical world.

Aikido training is not predominantly about fighting. Its prayer is much more about development of inner peace, creating outer peace through the cultivation of the spirit of reconciliation and through the quality of loving protection. Do not misunderstand: the practice can allow one to develop exceptional martial skills. The potential to effectively neutralize and subdue a violent attacker without injury is the reason the physical techniques are included in basic training for many Japanese police forces.

Just as it is possible to train in the physical aspect of the art without attention to the spiritual, it's possible to train in the spiritual aspect without practicing the external physical martial forms. The two do, however, complement each other beautifully in the spirit of growth and development.

The forms are a feedback system that allow what is happening in the hidden realms to surface visibly into the manifest realm. The practice makes one's relationship to the universe visible, awakening and refining the natural process of correction. The alive system corrects balance in response to feeling imbalance. When we enter into experience, we increase our awareness of tension, leading us to seek resolution in the back-and-forth that is like music. Harmonizing, adjusting, correcting, and resolving tension into harmony create the music, activating the dance of Aikido.

In Aikido, unifying the physical realm of awareness and Ki gives birth to the unified field out of which infinite techniques appear. Osensei called it *Takémusu Aiki*, which expresses creativity that gives birth to infinite form in every domain of function.

JIYU WAZA: QUESTIONING THE MYSTERY

In the traditional practice of Aikido, a student is introduced to the art through the sensei, or teacher, demonstrating a specific technique. The students repeat the form, imprinting it into muscle memory so it can be executed without thought. The physical realm is the tangible doorway for a beginner.

Waza is the Japanese term for "technique." *Jiyu waza* is the term for "free technique." The Japanese culture is highly structured, leaving little room for improvisation. In traditional study, Jiyu waza implies the freedom to apply any technique one has learned. In music that would be composition, learned for proprioceptive performance. Music includes exploration into another dimension, the improvisational process. Pure and applied science are somewhat analogous to improvisation and composition. Form and flow, knowledge and inquiry, all work together. The power of improvisation created all the forms, techniques, software programs, and compositions that exist. Composition relates to the known, improvisation the unknown. In Takémusu Aiki they complete each other, ever refining the cutting edge of possibility. Takémusu

Jiyu waza implies opening to the realm that creates technique in the moment: spontaneous, instantaneous creativity beyond forms that already exist or have existed—though it can and does include both.

Practice can strengthen a set of muscles and the neural pathways that trigger them, activating a given technique. When we are facing life-and-death challenge, seeking the safety of the strength and power developed through established techniques is an understandable strategy. Perfecting our technique proves valuable in situations of threat. It allows skillful application of techniques as one might develop the skill to use software programs.

The ability to see the shortcomings in a software application, when combined with the ability to write one that is more aligned with the needs of the moment, opens the possibility of creating new software appropriate to changing needs or conditions. Exploring principles enhances the power and freedom to use established programs or create new ones—whichever would better serve.

There are always unexpected challenges to face, and our response cannot be to prepare for all the specifics. Aikido, the power of improvisation, opens up confluence with the infinite mystery. In his writings, the founder cautions against getting lost in technique and operating from the fragmented world of matter. He emphasized repeatedly the centrality of standing on the floating bridge of heaven, unifying the heavenly and manifest realms as a unified field. Aligning, allowing, and appreciating unifies the experience of self and the universe as one system, taking the recognition into functional experiential creativity.

The Kami designed the techniques so the movement would lead students back to the originating principle of resonant, universal harmony. Harmony, experientially remembering the single source out of which the diversity of the manifest realm appears, resolves conflict. The guidance of the Kami experientially unites attention with the single source, the divine animating principle that is the origin of all pattern and form.

Aikido transforms the seeming opposites of the wave particle duality into what might be termed wave-particle unity, an experience of the single source. It describes a formless study wherein techniques, actions, and creations in the manifest world appear out of an unformed flow of energy and dissolve back into the field of potential in the same time-space. The founder called it Takémusu Aiki, which might be translated as "the way of harmony with the divine spirit of infinite creativity."

The principles of Aikido—once absorbed, inculcated, and embodied—kinesthetically produce the spontaneous creation of innovative free technique. The founder said, in the art of peace there are no *kata*, fixed forms, or prescribed set movements. Feeling gives birth to movement. Rather than imposing a form already composed, kinesthetic feeling improvises spontaneous, confluent movement created in the moment out of no*thing*. By creating new learning in the moment, improvisation gives birth to new forms and previously unknown possibilities.

Takémusu Jiyu waza listens, allowing the energy to give birth to movement, doing whatever seems appropriate, right, and fitting in the moment. It allows expression interconnected with everything; free, formless improvisational movement; jazz. It does not matter how an action compares with a form from the past. Drawing on, yet free of all learned forms, the interplay is jazz.

Commonly, when most people walk in nature, they follow a path. Without the specific intent to seek creativity and improvisation, they default to taking a familiar route. The body, neural energy, and synaptic connection take an established pathway, usually without a thought. Explorers, especially the explorers in jazz, are drawn to dimensions that transcend established pathways. When the principles are absorbed, forms come into being and then dissolve. Standing on the floating bridge of heaven, they combine to play jazz-like, free-form, improvisational Aikido.

Jazz and freestyle training empower the creation of solutions that don't yet exist. Techniques naturally emerge in perfect relationship to the unfolding energy. Learning translates out of the dojo and into daily life. The outcome of practice develops enriched improvisational skills in every facet of life. The practice explores the wonder of improvisation itself. The nature of deepening study is that answers will produce or lead to new questions.

In jazz, feeling gives birth to music. In Aikido, feeling gives birth to movement. Birthed out of the emptiness of the shining void, classical science, when it positions attention while standing on the floating bridge of heaven, and releases a fixed position on what it knows, opens to quantum mechanics—as the realm of music opens to jazz, and the martial arts open to the realization of love.

NOTICING AND CHOOSING

Improvisation can't be taught. It comes out of the unknown, out of the unexpected. That is what creativity means. There is nothing creative about the expected. A student can be taught the known forms and guidance offered; they can be encouraged toward open exploration of the unknown. Then, as they open to the unknown, entering into action and unifying thought and feeling, creativity happens . . . or not.

The funny thing is, it *does* happen, because self is connection to infinite creativity. Presence in the spirit of reconciliation is the recipe for improvisation to improve joy. Improvisation, which from the larger perspective is what creation is, emerges out of the wonders of the one system, the single source. Entering the unknown off the line, breathing wonder, improvisation is the natural expression of the creative force of the universe. The mysterious force of creativity, birthed out of a field of mystery, is as ubiquitous as the force driving the expansion of the universe. It flows everywhere, ceaselessly.

Creativity goes beyond technique; it is the expression of living in a spirit of harmony with the creative force of the universe. Spiritual practice opens to universal energies that lead to creativity beyond fixed identities or habituated thought patterns. An open spirit creates possibilities that a fixed identity, in its well-intentioned defensiveness, would never be willing to imagine let alone enter. By training to enter each experience in or with a harmonious relationship with Ki, we develop the courage and wisdom to negotiate the mysterious, changing universe in a positive spirit of loving harmony.

SPIRITUAL TRAINING AND THE SPIRALING OF CREATION

The word *spirit*, coming from a Latin root meaning "breath," is a term that probably has as many interpretations as interpreters. The Japanese word *kokyu*, also translated as "breath," could be more usefully understood as the force of spirit that activates the breath. Spirit might be understood as the between, the invisible essence, the activating principle that connects all matter, energy, and consciousness.

The word describes a quality of the energy of a being, as when someone says "good spirits," "a very spirited horse," or "into the spirit of the party." *Attitude* is a related word but lacks the power of creation implied in the word *spirit*. Spirit includes a larger domain, a connection to the forces that source creation in its totality. Though less mystical than *spirit*, the term *energy* may offer another window into the force that creates everything.

Spirit, *inspiration*, and *spiral* all share the same root. Life spirals. When the diaphragm activates breathing, air moves not in a straight line but in a spiraling pattern, the way leaves move in the wind. Spiraling appears in the way that water drains, the way nature unfolds—flowers in bloom, pinecones, trees—all of them form in a spiraling motion. Spiraling energy uncoils into creation. From a relative position, watching waves as they come above the surface, it looks like they are going up and down, whereas in reality they are spiraling through the ocean.

All of creation is a spiraling dance, from the shape as well as the movement of galaxies right down to the microbiological level of DNA. Solar systems are not circles as they appear in two-dimensional representations. Since the sun that they are orbiting is moving as part of the motion of galaxies, the whole system is a spiral in three-dimensional space. Just as a wire wound in spirals around an iron core makes a magnet, the spiraling movements of galaxies and solar systems travel-ing through space are also creating something comparable to magnetic fields of force, at the universal level.

Models of DNA molecules are pictured in a spiraling design. In one theory of the universe, physicists describe the basic form of matter as super-strings: winding, coiling strings of one dimension. When energy moves, there's a coiling and uncoiling spiral. Ki, universal energy, moves in spiraling, serpentine patterns that include the power of spirit, heart, and mind. These movements originate in yet-finer dimensions, but are already happening on Earth: the DNA double-helix spiral existed long before human history, long before anyone ever thought about universal movement; and it will exist long after.

Each aspect of a system—energy movement as well as the move-ments of the body and the movements of thought—teaches about the whole. The practice of feeling and blending with the spiraling energy of the universe is visible and tangible in the physical realm. Virtually every Aikido movement and technique uses spiraling movements.

The principle carries into the mental and spiritual realms; for example, we might describe someone as being "on an emotional spiral." Thought patterns spiral, as when an old idea comes around in a new way. Present and fluid, the spiraling, uncoiling, unfolding happens and everything evolves in relationship to it. As connection opens to the uni-versal spiral, its power becomes accessible.

Spiraling is organically connected with everything that's going on. Everything that's going on, is going on because it, the spiraling, is going on; and all this relates to what is meant by the word *spirit*. Everything manifests of spirit, which is always spiraling and uncoiling, enfolding and unfolding. Harmony with the flow of energy connects attention with the domain of existence where spirit is the primary dynamic. Spiritual training develops fluid temperament, the ability to live *in and with* a chosen spirit, exploring an unknown, incomprehensible infinity.

CONCLUSION

INTO UNCERTAINTY:
THE POWER OF WONDER

Observed through one slit, light appeared as a particle. When someone got curious enough to add a second slit and observed the changing pattern, the story changed. Looked at through two slits, suddenly the pattern that was seen and the story that was told turned virtually one hundred and eighty degrees from the well-established, firmly held conception of matter and energy as separate and distinct entities. Around the early twentieth century, countering millennia of scientific credence, science made up a new story where light was either both matter and energy, or something else altogether. In the quantum world where matter dissolves into energy, certainty dissolves into probability, and probability dissolves into uncertainty.

In the alive system's attempt to comprehend the mystery, to learn, to simply feel better and negotiate life's challenges more effectively, imagination attempts to explain and understand the incomprehensible through simplifying the world into stories. In the Christian Bible, John 1:1 begins with the phrase, "*In the beginning was the Word*, and the Word was with God, and the Word was God." The Dhammapada (Pāli; Sanskrit: धर्मपद), a primary Buddhist text, teaches that life of today is based on the thinking of yesterday, and life of tomorrow will be based on the thinking of today. Developing in the same time cycle with quantum mechanics, Aikido, and jazz, the premier work of psychology and psychiatry in the mid-twentieth century established, explored, and expanded the healing power of story for improving the quality of an individual's life.

Story, seeing patterns and making meaning out of experience, is as fundamental an activity of human consciousness as breathing is to corporal existence. The unified field of breathing in and breathing out produces and sustains aliveness, as night and day merge one into the other in the eternal flow of time. Similarly, unformed experience and experience filtered through description create, inform, and complete each other.

Knowledge, molding life experience, develops through the back-and-forth between experience and meaning-making, each iteration transforming the kaleidoscopic process. Words and thought shape each other, and both hold meaning and structure. At the same time, in a world of relativity, words are fluid, living entities. In the sea of consciousness, they mutate and evolve, taking story along for the ride.

From the time of primitive thought, when we inferred reality by interpreting the shadows on the cave wall, the stories of science, ontological study, and spiritual practice have sought direct experience of reality. Buddhist terminology describes it as *satori*, transcendent enlightenment. The Sanskrit term *nirvana* implies freedom from maya, illusion; a blissful dissolution of identity, fixed-thought systems, and karmas, opening into pure experience. In the Judeo-Christian-Islamic lineage, story describes ultimate reality with a variance of themes like heaven, a state of grace, and union with the divine or knowing God. In the world of science, enlightenment and God exist as verifiable truth.

From a geocentric world to a multi-galactic cosmos balancing probability with uncertainty, stories have imagined and negotiated the unpredictable experiment of life. By something as simple as slightly altering the experiment, what had been assumed true now appeared the opposite. Simply looking through two slits instead of one caused the story to change. And as the story changes, it changes the world.

IMAGINATION, CENTRAL CORE, AND THE PREFRONTAL CORTEX

Whereas virtually every other surviving species lives as creatures did before humans took form, the power of imagination, interconnected with the development of the prefrontal cortex, has transformed and amplified human ability and taken humanity into a dramatically new and different world. Things previously beyond imagination are currently commonplace in human existence. Creativity, and the communication and cooperation it engenders, transported humanity out of the caves into the blinding light of technological advancement.

Rather than stopping or slowing, the pace and impact of technology continue to increase exponentially. The uniquely human power of creating story, of imagination, of connecting thoughts and forming ideas, is a double-edged sword. The word for *crisis* in Chinese ideograms combines the symbols for "danger" and "opportunity." On the threshold of a crisis, the speed and power of the development of technology can threateningly outpace the development of the spirit or quality of the beings who are employing the technology.

The prefrontal cortex, by sending ideas back to central processing to be reconsidered, initiates the process of wonder and inquiry. The resonance back and forth between the prefrontal cortex and the rest of the brain evolves thought beyond the binary reptilian response of competition for survival and the rigidity of mammalian thinking fixed by first impressions. The forebrain, in challenging established pathways, allows human thinking to go beyond the assumptions of earlier brain function and past understanding, freeing life from habitual function, and instead generating spontaneous innovation.

Wonder, exploring the realm of truth, and seeking new information all disturb established structures of thought. Resisting the disturbance disconnects attention and inhibits growth, solidifying existing structures of thought and feeling. Certainty suffocates inquiry. Activation of the force of wonder that underlies development of the prefrontal cortex empowers neural connection, opening innovative possibilities.

FLOW

Increasingly the pace of life and the impact of change intensify pressure on structures of thought, ideologies of societies, and the emotional bonds of the entire species. Attention responds to the speed and stimulus of change along a continuum, either shutting down, withdrawing, resisting the flow of life force, or intentionally opening to harmony with the energy of the universe. One path, reactively polarizing in resistance, leads to discomfort, disconnecting from the source of divine wisdom, and thus diminishing the power of being. The other path, loving the challenge, turning on to it, and dancing into spiritual awakening, accesses its power.

Through repetition natural proclivities, feelings, beliefs, and attitudes, as well as other habitual patterns, materialize in the physical realm as synaptic pathways, consciously developing awareness or unconsciously reinforcing habituation. In the instant before experience becomes a circuit in the manifest world of matter and brain synapses, the magnetism of spirit attracts or repels the mystery. Once established, synaptic pathways that are reinforced through repetition will disappear into the fabric of personality. They go unnoticed, yet hold sway unless disturbed.

Spiritual exercises, practices for awareness, martial studies, art and dance, and esoteric schools that develop higher brain function all activate the prefrontal cortex, challenging past patterning that underlies present thinking, and creating a rich internal dialogue. Feeling, and bringing the aspects of thought and feeling into synchronicity, amalgamates aspects of being. Direct experience in the moment frees sufficient energy to restructure established synaptic pathways.

Uncertainty and wonder can water and nourish the seeds of inquiry, exploration, and dialogue. Intentionally experiencing disturbance and living into ambiguity will nurture the process of growth and development, crystallizing creativity into the wisdom to live life in a joy and wonder-fulfilling manner. When we increasingly shine the light of awareness on the distinction between direct experience and the meaning made from it, we enhance attention's ability to perceptively create story and lead to the external destination that calls from within.

ILLUMINATING THE PATH

The martial aspect of the art is first introduced in the most tangible dimension, through the physical forms. References in the teachings to the manifest realm, the techniques, and the physical aspects of brain development, all point to and reflect creative energies of a finer dimension. The founder spoke of the visible aspects of technique as "the dust after the action." The study uses the physical forms to explore and develop relationship with an original unseen causal force, a god or gods, underlying the creation of the visible hologram of reality.

As the movement of leaves makes the wind visible, the techniques make visible an energy path, guiding return to source. The martial study harmonizes with the power of intent, the Ki, the source of energy activating the motion of an attacker. In its universal alchemy, Aiki traces an experientially harmonious path from the manifest, to the hidden, and ultimately to creation's essential organizing dynamic. When the known dissolves into the divine origin, being experiences both self and the force of creation as a unified field. The dimensional shift of paying attention to feeling is less mystical than it sounds, and generates an experiential process with simple fundamentals.

The three domains of manifest, hidden, and divine can be distinguished in description and study, but doing so does not controvert the original underlying unity. The findings of scientific studies correspond to our physical experience, and harmonize with energy in finer dimensions of awareness, when they find an entrainment of brain waves, heartbeat, pulse, and breathing. Changes in the level of oxygen in the blood and the rate of absorption are all part of the process that show up physically, interpenetrating mystical visions, insights, and enlightenment experiences.

The beauty of the physical training is the tangible feedback available. Proper training, grounding the spiritual aspect of the process in harmony with the manifest domain, diminishes the delusional potential of deceiving oneself. The unified field may exist as a theory in science. In the way of harmony, a dimensional process opens us to the unity of the creative force and the creation, by means of experience.

FINER ENERGIES IN AN ENERGY UNIVERSE

The poetry of science terms every inexplicable occurrence or action with the words *force*, *field*, and *energy*. What science recognizes and labels as forces, fields, and energies, primitive societies explained by interpreting them as mystical beings, demons, and gods. As art and science expand, new discoveries can at first only be described through poetic application of archaic terms, because when we are looking into the future, neither the language nor the understanding that gives birth to evolving processes presently exists. Both aspects—creating meaning to understand, and the language that makes it possible—create each other in an ongoing spiral.

Life and every interrelated action, function, and skill manifest out of Ki, energy; though we are unable to know precisely what life and energy are. As if words could capture the infinite flow, whether it is described as life, energy, source, the force, the infinite, creativity, the mystery, creation, mother nature, random chance, the unified field, the unnamable, or the mind of God; and those are just *some* of the titles used in English. The emerging evidence increasingly continues to reflect and reinforce the postulate of a unified field. From multiple gods to monotheism, from things made of a hundred elements to all matter being energy, from a world of forces to unified field theory, the story continues to evolve.

Once activated, finer dimensions of awareness interact in a seemingly different world. Spiritual practices, and the act of paying attention to "feeling better," awaken a dimensional shift in consciousness, enriching the field of potential. The increasing energies of finer dimensions activate creative response to unfolding change, transforming fear into the harbinger of power.

Thinking about the mystery, everything seems ever more mystical. Thought, when unconnected to feeling, winds in on itself. Conversely, focusing attention into feeling the aliveness of being produces the experience of presence. The mystery gets less mysterious as it becomes a felt experience. The system opens. Energy flow increases. Life gets a little bit brighter. What can be seen changes, altering thought, meaning, and story.

In the increasing light of quantum mechanics, physics exists as if in another reality beyond classical science. Aiki magnetically unifies spirit, creating laser-like brilliance through the focus of intent. In that light, the world looks different. When shadows that appeared as threats transform into creative possibility, the strategies created are different. The outcomes are different. The brighter light of heightened consciousness increases comprehension of the universe, empowering an increasingly functional and enjoyable journey through life.

GROUNDED TO THE FLOATING BRIDGE

Life goes on in a familiar fashion, until that unpredictable moment when it does not. What will probably be happening tomorrow can be anticipated and prepared for based on experience. Yet the future remains uncertain. Until a prediction comes true, it is just a probability. In life, everyone faces the unknown. The quality of life is determined by *how* they face it.

To varying degrees, we can experience disturbance and a disruption of function both from facing the unexpected and from activating our energy for adaptation to change. In the rush of energy that drives us to act, should attention fail to notice and correct for the disturbance or startle reflex, strategy forms in haste and action is taken while we are upset, out of sorts, or in a state of un-readiness. Adrenaline, while enhancing our mental firing, clouds higher cognitive function and makes our mind's aim less precise. Conversely, deep concentration produces clarity of mind and slows our reflexes and firing. Getting ready starts with recognizing the need and correcting upset through experientially centering, grounding, and spiritually opening to allow energy to flow.

When well connected to ground, one can move easily in response to change, whereas on ice, movement is unsure and precarious. Grounded in one's central core of being, one can move functionally within the spiritual realms. Without ground, people slide around on emotional ice, feeding situations they never intended to, the repercussions of which take on a life of their own and go on long beyond any actual event.

Grounded being moves in appropriate relationship to unfolding creation. Returning to a centered, grounded, flowing state in response to the unexpected, before strategy and action take shape, is the critical fundamental in the process of reaching a desirable outcome. The outcome of applying the skills of both aiming and firing depends primarily on the process of getting ready, going from surprise, startle, and shock to instead centering experience in a calm, oxygenated, functional state of being.

When we are facing sudden, unexpected attack or any challenge in life, the subtlest, oft-overlooked aspect of the ready-aim-fire process— the stage of getting ready, of unifying the field of being—is the foundation of power. The first step in mastering the skills of self-defense or negotiating life is positioning the location of the center of attention in the center of power, the central core of aliveness and experience.

Standing on the floating bridge of heaven, positioning in one's best operating place, is the prerequisite step in correctly perceiving, precisely analyzing, incisively strategizing, and effectively executing desired action. By consciously relocating the center of attention to where it feels more at home, we positively influence mental and emotional state, or mood. Flexibility, adaptability, and innovative creativity—or the lack thereof—pivotally shape the quality of an individual's experience, and collectively, that of a society of individuals.

In a world of endless flow, the practice and quintessential skill affecting the value and quality of life is the skill of religiously aligning in a harmonious relationship with the dynamic energy of the universe. Less mystical than it sounds, harmonizing with the universal energy that emerges through the alive system as Ki is as simple as focusing attention on feeling better. Mastery continually relocates attention in relationship to the pulse and pressure of each energy rush, so perception, strategy, and action operate from a centered, grounded, flowing state of balanced equanimity.

The power of presence under pressure in an emergency also has value when translated to the rest of life, which is less of an emergency. What is dramatically true in an emergency, and true in less noticeable ways in negotiating daily tasks of life, is that getting ready, centering, and standing on the floating bridge of heaven all locate attention in the power of joy, which emanates from the harmony of love.

The quality of intention, the spirit of the moment, and the quality of being write the story of competition for survival or cooperation for elegance. When the twin forces of creation—masculine-feminine, yin-yang, mind-body, thinking-feeling, attention and experience—unify, spirit's innate tonality of love radiates, giving birth to a world of peaceful reconciliation.

The gifts of love, harmony, and joy let us bravely face whatever the gods offer, and transform the cacophony of chaos into the music of the spheres, the joy of life made manifest. Aikido cultivates a spirit of enthusiastically flowing into "the great becoming isness" in the face of a life-and-death threat, which, taking the long view, describes the challenge that daily life eventually offers.

POSITIONING LOCATION

A surfer turns the potential energy of a wave into the kinesthetic energy of a ride by adjusting location, position, and attitude in harmonious relationship to the ever-changing motion as it unfolds—in other words, going with the flow. Tourists washed off the beach by big waves have drowned. Yet at the same time, in the same waves, in the same ocean, surfers are having the ride of their life.

Moving in harmony with the momentum of an attack neutralizes its force. Theoretically, one might move in tandem with the center of the eye of a hurricane until the hurricane depletes, and in this way neutralize any negative effect from it. Peace lives in the central core of the hurricane. Things seem normal. The sun is shining. The birds are flying. Yet beyond the edge of the eye, in the storm, life is an altogether different experience.

Harmonious relationship translates emotionally as well as physically. As the power of a hurricane generally depletes over dry land, anger, allowed to express itself unprovoked and given the gift of empathic attention, gradually dissipates. In an emotional hurricane, listening to understand while grounding the energy of the vortex, empathizing with feelings without getting caught up in them or adding to them, is dry land. Listening to someone else's pain potentially helps another to listen and thus to bring the aspects of self into unification.

When someone loses it, creative dialogue cannot take place until they find it. Negative affect generally represents internal pressure from surging energy flow, unexpressed or resisted in some form. Repressing, disregarding, or projecting feelings, or listening to a part of something without the context of the whole relationship, causes beings to fragment individually and collectively. In the magnetic presence of the strong force of a grounded, "centered" central core, eccentric behavior realigns.

When full expression of the concerns that underlie any resistance is absorbed by listening with attention, the field of energy transforms. Energy lost to resistance returns to its natural course. When people listen to each other as parts in the symphony, different but complimentary, the world opens. Opening to the incomprehensible, listening, and living into the unknown in a love of wonder, all return fragments into holistic understanding. When the unknown is received, the harmony of the larger system emerges. Creativity finds its way back into the dialogue.

When a spirit of listening and harmony is present, difficult conversations resolve and deepen the relationships between individuals, as well as unifying aspects within an individual. Emotional disturbance and pain or discomfort in the physical domain, when listened to, speak for electrical signals and chemicals. But when resisted, the sensations are just pain and discomfort. Paying attention—listening in the dimension of feeling, absorbing the signals and chemicals as information and guidance that lead into a larger system—changes the relationship. Listening internally as well as externally shifts state of mind, creating the story that unfolds.

Triangulating a coherent relationship of the individual with the totality will unlock creativity's hidden potential. Creativity, the skill of spontaneous improvisation, opens the possibility of enthusiastically surfing life's ubiquitous waves in an ever-changing universe. One can surf in the same ocean where the tourists are drowning, or harmonize in a world where conflict is the norm, for though the ocean, the world, and the externals of life may be the same, the quality of consciousness changes perception, strategy, function, and the world one experiences and brings into creation.

As the speed, frequency, and magnitude of change intensifies, the ability to surf the cosmos increases in value and consequence. Generally, surfing requires paddling out through the waves, which push one back toward shore. When we enter the experience of cosmic energy that is self, the waves of emanating radiance tend to push attention outward toward external focus. Continually returning to center, refining our ability to focus into the finer dimensions, is the process of the practice.

Precision practice produces extraordinary outcomes. The results the process produces are the dust after the action. For those who seek power to create a positive spirit and to elevate consciousness to the highest levels, focus on mastering the fundamentals is essential. Training in the way of harmony prioritizes standing on the floating bridge of heaven, positioning in best operating place, the driver's seat of being. This is the fundamental and primary skill, regardless of what one is aiming at, the task to be executed, or the destination sought.

The practice is staying with the process. Interest in results, positive or negative, magnetically distracts attention's focus from continually returning. Shortly, amnesia sets in, obscuring the fundamental principle that the quality of results comes from continually, intentionally focusing attention into experience. Outcome is important, but it is achieved by successfully negotiating the stretch of road one is driving at the moment. Training returns attention to the process, to feeling, and to unifying attention and experience.

Drawing on the energy of challenges—the waves, the force of a life-threatening attack, the winds of change, or the dynamics of diversity—transforms resolution, enhancing innovative solutions. Heightened perception in the realm of the spirit, through galvanizing precision in feeling location and adjusting position, can map and light the path to completion of life's bestowed mission.

Through the charm of every subatomic particle, the human spirit expresses itself as the portal to an expansive, mysterious force. The beauty in a sunset can take attention back to the infinite. Return to source calms the spirit, allowing a transparent reflection of the cosmic field. Negative feelings and situations still exist, but cosmic surfers, intentionally loving the challenge of riding the waves of change, experience a different world.

FEELING: THE UNIFIED FIELD EXPERIENCE

Feeling may be the most undervalued word in the English language. Feeling, the foundational determinant in the quality of one's life experience, activates the power of life to satisfy its needs and complete whatever quest the radiant magnetism of an individual draws to itself. Attentively listened to, the sound of feeling guides attention, increasing access to power emanating from central core, and creating a benevolent, reinforcing cycle.

Absent connection with feeling, thought isolates us, instead reinforcing habitual behavior. Once we are accustomed to a posture, facial expression, attitude, or a level of muscle tone, it feels normal and correct—as do systems of thought and belief. It can feel quite different to relax into the flow of aliveness, to release established energy patterns into appreciating formless experience. This feeling, even in infinitely small increments, may be identified as strange and as such, resisted.

Achieving harmony with the energy means practicing how to listen to disturbance—even and especially seeming discomfort—for information beyond immediate reactions or first sensations. Whether the sensations of feeling at first seem pleasant or unpleasant is not the significant information. Value lies in listening, which alone allows decoding the guidance toward feeling better.

To love the feeling of aliveness is central because aliveness, by its predilection, guides life to its completion. Reconnecting attention with the experience of source, when practiced religiously through feeling, brightens the power of being in every facet. A spirit of harmonizing, absorbing, and drinking the nourishing energy of aliveness empowers one to rise courageously, facing life's unexpected challenges as opportunities.

Feeling better, the ultimate mission of every goal of every strategy of every action, is less a choice than a hunger of life. Physical hunger is a tangible aspect of life's longing. Spiritual hunger is not satisfied by material things. The urge, the desire of aliveness, and the longing toward nourishment call in subtler voices, in finer dimensions, in all three domains. The calling of spirit has its own fulfillment to satisfy. The spirit is nourished courageously by following the path of joy and interest toward the destination of harmony with the mystery. When we listen to feeling, we naturally move toward feeling better, harmonious, aligned, original, and authentic. Accessed repeatedly, this listening becomes familiar. And with increased familiarity, it becomes home base, the quality on which life is founded.

Aiki, feeling better, experiencing and expressing the divine connection of original self, is more important to quality of life than scientific knowledge or religious doctrine. Though either may contribute, both are a means to an end goal. Feeling better leads to, and comes from, intentionally and directly experiencing the magnetic radiance of the strong force of central core, in harmonious relationship with universal Ki.

The quest for a beautiful world of personal freedom, freedom of mind, freedom of being, and freedom of spirit, is first an internal transformation. Bringing the world into balance, neutralizing or transforming negativity, is a process that emanates from within. The transmission of the power of harmony comes from living it. Sharing awareness happens magnetically through activating the process. In a state of harmonious radiance, little needs to be said beyond what is uniquely appropriate and incisively aligned with the moment.

Aiki takes place in finer energy dimensions as intention takes form, before conscious thought or neural signals, and long before visible action. When the central core and the larger field experientially balance, the heart opens, creatively enhancing life. Without the connection to the radiance of Ki, the gravitational pull of the past retards entry into the present. Joy, an evocative feeling, frees exploration to move beyond thought structures of the past. The past serves the future in a stream of positive, radiant energy, courageously facing the unknown.

Feeling into the pulse of the breath harmonizes life's rhythms with the pulse of creation. The impulse to breathe, when one listens to it, intones the universal overtone series of joy. Taking a deep breath almost always feels better. Two or three practically come with a guarantee. Even a simple sigh moves attention some increment in the right direction. With each increment, attention focuses into the experience of the central core, taking us one step on the thousand-mile journey.

Remembering peak experiences that one is fond of is often enough to magnetically trigger the shift in location, causing the hormonal mixture that is loved when it releases, because it feels better. One can simply intentionally appreciate experience more—that is, feel better—by intoning ever-finer harmony with the universe, thus inducing feeling better. Feeling into experience better, heightening sensory acuity into ever-finer dimensions, feels even better.

THE WAY OF LISTENING

The divine or creative force appears in life through the enlivening energy that flows into, through, and as the alive system. Whether one listens to the counsel of feeling or resists the energy's message establishes the seed crystal, foundational cornerstone, or fundamental heart-forming life experience. Listening in the realm of the spirit, recognizing and allying with rather than ignoring or suppressing disturbance, relinks attention and experience.

The concept of religion implies reconnecting to the divine source. A religious person was once someone who practiced reconnecting repeatedly, religiously. In current usage, the term *religious* is more commonly used to describe those who believe a specific doctrine on faith, thus surrendering doubt and inquiry. *Prayer*, in common usage, has come to describe asking for favors. *Prayer* in a more original usage meant the process of re-establishing connection to the infinite.

The practice of prayer, or religiously opening into the incomprehensible, dissolves the known, reconnecting experiential union with the mystery. In contradistinction to holding rigid beliefs, prayer and religion as ways of opening to the infinite unknown offer religiously repeated dissolution of identity into unification, relinking with the divine as self.

Divine, beyond any fixed belief systems or religious implications, rather describes creative power transcending present human perception and understanding. Prayer as a portal relinking to the divine, returning the personal to its original oneness with the universal, transmutes longing into the gift of humility and the joy of honoring the sacred.

Regardless of the lineage, art, or path one takes in exploring life's fulfillment, victory in feeling better, creating story out of harmonious creativity, frames the warrior's challenge. Harmoniously unifying attention and experience into creative power, experientially dancing the vitality of aliveness into joy, defines the spiritual quest. Through the slight alteration of adding a second slit to the design of the experiment, questioning the composition of light, the universe of matter was transformed into energy. Metaphorically, Aikido offers a second slit in life's experiment in the realm of the spirit.

THE BIRTH OF CREATIVITY

Discoveries in the quantum world completely transformed the world of technology and introduced human consciousness to previously imperceptible dimensions of energy beyond understanding, comprehension, even imagination. In the transition from earlier forms of their disciplines, Aikido, quantum mechanics, and the infusion of jazz into mainstream music around the same time, all shattered the previous stories of their lineages.

As quantum mechanics transformed the world of physics, Aikido's exploration encompassed a previously unknown dimension beyond the concept of traditional martial arts. Aikido offered another paradigm from which to see experience and create the stories that perpetuate the unfolding. Religiously seeking the eye of the hurricane, centering the focus of attention into experience in the face of pressure, is the challenge, the practice, and the gift of Aiki, the spiritual science of joy. Aikido, as the founder repeatedly stated in so many ways, was not about defeating others. The mission of Aikido is creating a world where that was not even a question.

In Tibetan Buddhism, there is a practice known as the *chöd* rite. It is also called "the short path," due to its extreme speed and effectiveness for attaining enlightenment in a single night. The Tibetan word chöd means "to cut off"—to cut through narcissism and fixed identity to find original self, experiencing reality free of karmas from the past. Chöd in this context means to slay the confusion of the "I" or identity, revealing self, the essence of being, as a unified field with the divine source.

The rite is usually performed where the bones of the dead have been left to decay. The practitioner, entering directly into the energies, summons the demons blocking the path to nirvana. Body, persona, and identity are bravely offered to be consumed by the demons to satisfy and sanctify their spirits. Through the transformative process of yielding the known and allowing it to be assimilated back into the energies of the universal field, history and identity dissolve. Only the immutable remains.

The whisperings of the technology of quantum Aikido offer human consciousness feedback as well as an entry point into experiential exploration of the mystery. Through love and courage, surrendering separation, and dissolving barriers, the essence of being assimilates the powers and energies, which at first appear as monsters and demons. The power of harmony intentionally absorbs, transforms, and applies the energy of change. Once the energies recognize unification with the totality, negative feelings, fear, and enmity transform into love and friendship. Energies that were once upsetting, even terrifying, become allies empowering life's journey.

The unified field experience of locating the focus of the center of attention into the center of experience is Aiki's chöd rite. The simple internal alignment of Aiki, each pulse seemingly so insignificant, in the collective transforms the field of potential and the world that manifests out of it.

In the unified field of spirit, another dream, another world, a different universe is possible. In a funny way, to create the story of a world in harmony with a changing universe may turn out to be as simple as metaphorically creating an experiment with three slits. Until that happens, what story might be told and what world might unfold hover on the threshold of imagination . . . calling.

APPENDIX
QUANTUM POETRY

A Poem by Gary David

In the unfolding of a story of a life,
It inevitably reaches its limits.
One stands at the cusp of a vast and unknown landscape.
The quiet dawn of realization—
A soft whisper—
That says there is more to this existence
Than we ever learned to believe.
This is the call of a new orientation,
A beckoning toward uncharted territories
   of heart and mind.

To learn the way into this new orientation
Is to dance in the unknown in a rhythm of change
And let it guide on the edge of not knowing,
Not in a journey of miles,
But of perceiving, accepting, committing,
trusting—A voyage inward, To the depths of being,
And outward,
To the far horizons of human becoming.
Here, change is the only constant—
   In the moving currents of meaning.

Consider the shift in perspective:
The first light of dawn
Breaking over a weary night.
Familiar contours of knowing
Suddenly lit anew.
Landscapes once fallen into
The Valley of Perceptual Skill,
Are bathed in a new light,
Revealing landscapes beckoning
    exploration

This new vantage point
Invites a different kind of participation—
To question,
To consider,
To accept the mute assumptions of
All previous learning
with unclouded heart.
To keep what stabilizes
And to seek freedom
    from there.

As the new terrain unfolds,
Each step in the dance—
A movement toward greater degrees of freedom
To meet the limits of life on Earth.
Old scripts fall away like autumn leaves,
Making room for what has not yet spoken,
For seeds of possibility rooting in the fertile soil
Of open attention.
This shift—The dance of life's endless capacity
    for renewal.

And there in the raw beauty of
An emotional order
Rooted in the biological core of affect
We learn to ride the waves of change
Like a seasoned sailor
Heeding directions beneath the wind.
This adjustment Is not for the faint of heart
It is a pilgrimage to where the fires of transformation
* burn brightest.*

Then, as the heart composes new music,
Minding reaches—
Like the branches of an ancient tree
Stretching toward the light
Of the acceptance underling understanding
That illuminates, reveals.
Cognition, no longer distant,
Unfolds like petals of insight blooming
In the warmth
* of purposeful feelings.*

In this new world,
Arises a being that becomes signal—
A quiet beacon drawing others
Who resonate to the same frequency.
Forging connections that transcend
The social conventions
Of past stages of human development
It's the shaping of a new participation,
A shared narrative written in the language of the soul
* something more than reason.*

And finally—in the sanctity of quiet movement,
Transformation reveals itself
As an evolution of the self
Beyond the tight fit of ego,
Embracing the unspeakable
With the speakable.
It is a metamorphosis where
The universal is found
In the particulars
    of immediate experience.

This is the purpose
of a new orientation:
awakening
inside the dream
once learned through the voices and eyes of others.
To rise
from the ashes
of the known,
and move into the dawn
of what is still
    learning to be human.

Here,
We are both map and territory,
seeker and found,
the never ending dive
between feeling, question,
and response.
invitation to dance in the unknown
Wearing the clothing of the past in a
joyful, exciting, and sometimes fearful
    dancing in the dark.

A Poem by Stephen Samuels

This is a poem . . . well to me it is. The rhyme is something you will have to discover yourself.

Water is a miracle. Consider first that it arrived on earth, a molecule at a time, delivered by fragments of asteroids and comets over billions of years, until there was enough of it to be what we experience now as oceans, and rivers and lakes, and rain and clouds, and the fog on the mirror in your bathroom when you come out of a hot shower.

We take it for granted, but without it, we and most everything else would not be around.

Science tells us our bodies are about seventy percent water. Keep that in mind.

When you look around at your world, you see living things and stuff, but you don't usually think you are seeing mostly water. In that way, we might consider it the invisible part of all we see.

Until quite recently, science held a view of the Universe that comes from our intuitive observations of explosions. That is, stuff flies outward from the center of the explosion at great speed, and eventually slows down and stops moving. Science thought the Universe, and all that stuff, did the same. The accepted view was that eventually all the galaxies and other stuff in the Universe would keep expanding, while the rate of expansion became slower and slower until at some point it would stop. But then, they decided to test that with measurements.

What they found was shocking.

First, they found that all the stuff they could see, both with visible light and invisible light, did not account for the movements and behaviors of galaxies. So they came up with the idea that there must be more matter than can be seen. They called this Dark Matter. That helped explain a bit more of what was being observed.

But then they measured the rate of expansion, expecting to discover how much it was slowing down, and expecting to predict when exactly it would stop.

Shocking again: it is not slowing down. In fact, it is going faster and faster.

And, this could only mean one thing. There has to be some previously unimagined (for us, that is) fuel or power for this increasing rate of expansion.

They named this Dark Energy. It can't be seen, nor otherwise detected, hence the name Dark. But it is everywhere, ever present, and just "doing its thing." It is only "noticed" by the effect it produces.

And when they do the math to calculate how much Dark Energy there must be to power the expansion of all the visible and invisible matter, it turns out to be about seventy percent of the Universe.

Does that rhyme for you? It does for me.

INDEX

ABOUT THE AUTHOR

RICHARD MOON began formal study of Aikido in 1971 with Robert Nadeau Sensei—a personal student of the founder of the art of Aikido, Morihei Ueshiba Osensei. Richard has studied numerous martial arts, including Cheng Hsin, Tai Chi, and boxing with world champion Peter Ralston. He trained in Capoeira with three-time world heavyweight champion Mestre Acordeon Bira Almeida. He has studied and taught yoga since 1963. Richard studied dance with John Graham and improvisational theater with The Committee. A lifetime student across a broad spectrum of music, he has studied with many masters in many styles, including classical guitar with George C. Economides, Indian ragas and voice with flautist G. S. Sachdev of the Ali Akbar College of Music, and jazz at the California Jazz Conservatory. Richard has also performed in numerous blues and rock bands over many decades.

As a partner with Chris Thorsen in an Aikido-based consulting firm, Richard has coached executives and their teams in the corporate realm, helping them to develop dynamic presence, inspired leadership, and collective intelligence. Using issues of conflict as sources of power, the firm has worked with groups to facilitate communication and creativity, to mediate, and to solve problems through the power of extraordinary listening. Richard's work combining Aikido and dialogue in a sophisticated marriage was enriched by his study of dialogue with David Bohm and nonviolent communication with Marshall Rosenberg. Richard has worked internationally, applying the principles of Aikido in mediation and international peace building through work done in Cyprus, Bosnia-Herzegovina, and around the Pacific Rim.

For more information and instructional videos that focus on consciousness and awareness studies, visit Richard's YouTube channel: @moonsensei.